To Carolyn Walls

Whose constant aid, unfailing sense of humor, and unchangeable faith in our favorite baseball heros are priceless boons to this associate.

Cliff Buttelman

Nov. 8, 1962

WILL EARHART
TEACHER
PHILOSOPHER
HUMANITARIAN

Copyright © 1962

Portions previously copyrighted in 1927, 1930, 1931, 1933, 1934, 1937, and 1958

by the

Music Educators National Conference

Library of Congress Catalogue Number 62-12796

Printed in the U.S.A.

Price $3.50

A STEADFAST PHILOSOPHY

A selection of papers written by Will Earhart dating from 1914, including his last writings, hitherto unpublished, with some personal reflections by disciples and pupils of this great man of music education.

Prepared by the Music Educators National Conference, a Department of the National Education Association, 1201 Sixteenth Street N.W., Washington 6, D. C.

EDITOR'S FOREWORD

During the last years of his fruitful and always vigorous life, Will Earhart was approaching total blindness. With his alert mind and with the constant aid and support of Mrs. Earhart, only a few close friends really understood the extent of the visual handicap. During this period, to the everlasting credit of Mrs. Earhart, the latest writings, which appear as Section One of this book, came into being and were made available for publication by the Music Educators National Conference. With this portion of the content, the editor, by authority of the Music Educators National Conference Board of Directors, has combined in Section Two papers and addresses taken from issues of the Conference Journals of Proceedings and Yearbooks, dating from 1914.

Section Three is mainly devoted to biographical or related material. Acknowledgment is made of contributions by Felix E. McKernan and Hubert S. Conover.

The former, *Will Earhart, His Life and Contributions to Music Education,* is Mr. McKernan's report of a graduate study sponsored by the University of Southern California School of Education, and completed in 1960.

Mr. Conover's contribution, *Memories of Will Earhart,* written for the 50th anniversary reunion, September 24, 1960, of the Richmond, Indiana, High School Class of 1911, reflects personal recollections beginning with the author's early school days when Mr. Earhart was supervisor of music in the Richmond Public Schools, 1908 to 1912.

Other content of Section Three is self-explanatory.

For the benefit of those to whom the equivalent of a table of contents would be helpful, a complete listing of titles of articles, years, and page references is provided (page 143). Also included (pages 141-142) is a general bibliography, listing alphabetically by authors most of the books referred to by Mr. Earhart in articles printed in Section Two.

A personal note here may serve to explain the selection of the material which forms the second section of the book, and also to support the choices made.

It was in the years somewhat prior to the employment of this writer in 1930 as Executive Secretary of the Music Educators National Conference that his first contact was made with Will Earhart, then director of music in the public schools of Richmond, Indiana. The incidental meeting occurred when a chance walk past the Richmond High School led to an interview with the conductor of the high school orchestra which was being rehearsed. Perhaps incredulity is the word to introduce at this point. Here was what appeared to be a complete symphony orchestra, with a complement of instruments such as was almost unknown to the visitor except from hearsay and exceedingly rare visual-auditory experiences with orchestral ensembles of symphonic status—none of which, to his knowledge, then existed in any high school or small community.

Thus began one of the most valued friendships ever the good fortune of any person to share. From that time on—and long after Will Earhart had moved from Richmond to become director of music in Pittsburgh in 1912—it was my privilege to be the beneficiary of the Earhart counsel, guidance and wisdom.

The title-page phrase, "A Steadfast Philosophy," was impressed upon the editor when reviewing papers and addresses, spanning a period of more than forty years, from which could be selected material suitable for Part Two of this book. The perusal reflected so many things reminiscent of contacts with Will Earhart—in conferences and personal interviews as well as in Research Council meetings and in committee or informal discussions in which he participated—that, indeed, there were instances when the editor could not discriminate between what he had only read and what he had one time, at least, actually heard Mr. Earhart say.

I am content if those of our friends in education who did not know Will Earhart as so many of us did, will, through this slim but rich volume, share in some degree the advantage which was ours.

CLIFFORD V. BUTTELMAN

SECTION ONE

VALUE OF MAN'S
NON-UTILITARIAN INTERESTS

I

THE ROOTS OF MUSIC APPRECIATION

II

WHAT IS MUSIC FOR?

III

CONGENITAL AND CHANGING ACQUIRED INTERESTS

This section comprises the three papers Mr. Earhart desired to have published as his final and climaxing statement to his friends and colleagues of the music education field. The decision to expand the publication by adding Sections Two and Three was made after Mr. Earhart's death.

VALUE OF MAN'S NON-UTILITARIAN INTERESTS

Author's Preface to Section One

A MORE FULLY DESCRIPTIVE TITLE for this little monograph would have been "Value of Man's *Preoccupation* with Non-Utilitarian Interests." The word "preoccupation" is likely to suggest long-continued and deep absorption of attention, whereas it may be brief, even momentary, and be comparatively shallow. Brevity of experiences, however, need not connote shallowness, inasmuch as one glimpse of transcendent beauty may leave an impression that remains in memory for a lifetime. Whether the impression is of the widow's mite's value or is colossal, it blends into the total of all other experiences and purifies and uplifts this spirit of man by that much. —W.E.

[The foregoing is verbatim from the original manuscript by Mr. Earhart, prepared when it was his expectation that what appears here as Section One would be published as a separate small book.]

I. THE ROOTS OF MUSIC APPRECIATION

> *While this part discusses a limited area of musical experience, it at the same time predicts a general outlook which is further expanded in the parts II and III.* —W.E.

THE SEARCH for a fundamental basis for teaching music appreciation may best be guided by an attempt to answer three questions. Since 1900, when I first organized and taught formal high school courses in music appreciation at Richmond, Indiana (where we called the subject The Critical Study of Music), those questions have beset me with increasing urgency. The questions are these: (1) What is there in music to be appreciated? (2) What is the nature of appreciation? (3) What is its value to human life?

Any attempt to answer these questions adequately leads us far. For appreciation of music, although primarily a subject for aesthetic study, lies also, with respect to our response to tone and tonal discourse, in the field of psychology; and, with respect to its value in life, in the field of philosophy. When inquiry has been directed to what could be observed from only one, or at most two, of these lookout stations, it has been likely to give us lamentably incomplete, distorted, or unreal views of music as we experience it. On the other hand, this same breadth placed almost insuperable difficulties in the way of treatment in a short paper, with the result that practical application of the theories advanced could hardly be indicated, and broad theories had to be outlined with perilous brevity.

I hold the glad belief that regardless of any doubts you may have about your courses in "music appreciation," you have done, and are doing increasingly, a magnificent job of developing appreciation of music. The evidence is all about you. It is seen in the number and stature of our symphony orchestras, the public response to fine concerts, and notably in the superb choruses, orchestras, and bands now developed in universities and high schools, and the beautiful singing and the playing of instruments now becoming general in elementary schools. Satisfaction over so great an achievement involving such vast numbers should surely offset any dissatisfaction you may feel over the results of your courses in music appreciation. Perhaps you have fallen victim to an astigmatism pointed out by a writer on education in a recent issue of a magazine. He deplored the tendency to believe that "the only way to learn anything is to take a course in it."

The second observation needed here requires longer discussion. It is made in order, so to speak, to provide a philosophical backdrop against which all succeeding entrants upon the stage must be seen.

A lack of proud satisfaction in the results of your work, and the value of these results to the world, may arise from the fact that the philosophy which supports the arts and makes clear their value is not the ruling philosophy in our society. Until teachers in the fields of the arts and humanities come to grips with this philosophical problem they are likely to remain inarticulate and even abashed in the presence of a wholly confident and highly articulate philosophical majority. Lovers of democracy are in similar need when, to confront the imposing structure of Marxian philosophy, they bring only a simple faith. They love democracy, but they urgently need also to know and hold in clearest conviction the truths of that system of thought upon which democracy is reared. So let us look at two diverse philosophies. We cannot, in this short space, do justice to either of them, and much that I say may be threadbare to you. Nevertheless, the resumé may not be useless.

The philosophy that chiefly characterizes and motivates our modern society is derived from Francis Bacon. In the Renaissance, men's minds were changed and quickened by a succession of momentous enlightenments and discoveries. One feature of that change was the shift of thought from the supernatural to the natural, from the heavens to the earth, from conception of a universe controlled by divine law to a physical one that obeyed mechanical physical laws, to a world that was consequently open to intellectual conquest, and, therefore, to physical control and manipulation by man. Jung puts the matter in a nutshell when he says: "The vertical outlook of the European mind was forthwith intersected by the horizontal outlook of modern times." This new outlook, carried to its furthest implications and systematized in his giant mind, became the philosophy of Francis Bacon, that has given rise to the vast scientific and technological achievements that have so improved man's lot—and now threaten to destroy him! But that philosophy was not all that Bacon believed and thought. It was, however, the great new thought, the thought needed to balance and complement that other conception of the universe which alone had dominated the minds of men, and which had left them in a state of what now appears to be practical ineptitude. That explains why Bacon pleaded it long and fervently, and mentioned his other beliefs only when he wished to define the limitations of his empirical philosophy.

Limitations! Our current thought does not recognize that there are any, or give attention to what Bacon said about them. What are they? The shortest answer is implicit in Bergson's terms, "the sciences of matter," and "the rational intellect." Such sciences probe matter, and such intellect discerns and formulates the physical laws which it obeys. Matter is known, we may observe further, to the physical senses, and the knowledge gained is knowledge of the physical world in which we live. Dewey terms this "a way of knowing," and it is a way that has achieved so much that some have come to think that it is the only way of knowing and that the realities it knows constitute the only reality.

But do we live only in a physical world? Is this way of knowing the only way, and does what it knows constitute the only reality? If so, those who talk about divine law, who meditate with St. Paul on faith, hope, and charity, or, with you, upon beauty, are dealing with unrealities. For these cannot be perceived by the physical senses, cannot be reached by the scientist's way of knowing, are not present for examination in any instrument in the scientific laboratory. It must be, then, that there are other realities, other things to be known, other ways of knowing. Bacon says explicitly that there are. Two brief quotations must suffice: At one place in *The Advancement of Learning* he writes: "If any man shall think by his inquiries after material things to discover the nature or will of God, he is indeed spoiled by vain philosophy—for thus the sense discovers natural things, while it shuts up the divine"; and later:

"Physics inquires into the efficient and the matter; metaphysics into the form and the end."

Science, then, cannot inform and guide us in moral and aesthetic matters, because it has not the prehensile apparatus, so to speak, with which to lay hold of immaterial things. Scientists, of course, may love and work passionately for the advancement of goodness and beauty—but that is because scientists, too, live in a world larger than that examined by their sciences. Strange that when the founder of natural science, Bacon, so clearly proclaimed its limitations, his modern disciples should not concede them. Thus John Dewey, in his *Reconstruction in Philosophy*, urges that the Baconian "way of knowing" be employed to improve the moral world as it has improved the material. James Bryant Conant, in the March 1948 number of the *Atlantic Monthly*, makes much the same plea. In answer to the charge that science does not discern values, he points to the beneficence represented by medicine, psychiatry, and cancer research, and pleads that science now turn its attention upon social betterment. Might science always be so beautifully employed! But the kindness, the human sympathy, are in the breast of the scientist and are not gathered from the phenomena he examines or the data he assembles. Only an idealistic philosophy that employs another way of knowing can come upon things unseen and recognize the purposes and values which those things hold.

The backdrop is surely completed, so let our questions enter.

"What is there in music to be appreciated?" As in all the arts, aestheticians find three factors, namely: Material, Form, and Expression. The material of music is commonly said to be Tone. Goodhart-Rendel, however, in an excellent little book, *Fine Art*, says that it is rather *ideas* of tone; because it is obvious that a piece of music can be composed without a single tone having been sounded, and another musician can read the score and thoroughly enjoy it—again without a tone having been sounded. The point has practical bearing because it emphasizes the great role of musical ideation. The music that delights us at a concert but which we do not remember is, of course, far from lost, because the high state of feeling aroused is in itself an experience that lives in us always. Nevertheless, music does its most for us when we hold in memory or create in our minds definite tonal images, with which we may commune or which may merely sing to us while we are otherwise occupied. That is why I so greatly emphasized so-called "creative music" in the Pittsburgh schools. It was the surest way to fill the minds of children with haunting tonal voices. So to dwell at times with a fascinating subjective content is, I believe, natural and beneficial to children as well as to older persons; for such moments mold our long years, while attention to the more clamorous objective world concerns only that more immediate "behavior," now so much studied.

You all know music, its psychology, and its aesthetics so well that I will speak only on phases of these that appear to have been insufficiently emphasized or to need more careful qualification. One such phase we are even now discussing; namely, the Material of an Art—in our case, Tone—as a factor in aesthetic response. Santayana pleads the power of material in all the arts with such eloquence that when Reid quotes a sentence from the plea he alludes to it as "a purple passage"; and Gurney certainly does full justice to our material, Tone, in his monumental book, *The Power of Sound*. Nevertheless, our general conception of Tone, and the nature and value of our response to it, appear to me in need of expansion.

First, let us remember that hearing, as developed from the "shake-sensations," is a short-distance notifier, and is consequently closer to our emotions—is more startling, more intimate—than sensations to the long-distance notifier, the eye. Tone is also the one exclusive and distinguishing possession of music. All the arts have Form and Expression, and all have rhythm. This is not to say that rhythm is not an outstanding feature of music (nowhere else, indeed, does rhythm attain the multitudinous variety of patterns possible in concerted music), but only to say that rhythm is not a distinctive possession of music. It may be seen as well as heard—for instance, in flashing light-beacons; felt, on skin and in muscles; and it is not, like Tone, a distinct ear-sensation, but, as a form of sound, reverberates throughout the whole neuromuscular system, impelling muscular response. As bearing upon appreciation, especially among young children whose concept of music and responsive attitude toward it should be rightly shaped, this is important—for it is frightfully easy to develop their attention and response to rhythm to the point where they become deaf to the real voice of music itself. That is why music for dancing or for marching does not seek the charm and pliancy of tone characteristic of music that is to be listened to. Jaques-Dalcroze, since he is an artist, treats rhythm in music in the only wise way, because, with him it is completely fused with form and expression in an artistic whole to which the hearer sensitively responds. Debasement takes place only when, as still happens in some kindergartens and elementary schoolrooms, the children are shaken out of absorption in the whole, and respond only to the rhythmic skeleton. Understand, please, that I want children to play, shout, stamp their feet, exercise their bodies. I am merely pointing out that these are not practices that lead specifically to appreciation of music.

We know that Tone engages only the senses. Since children are in a sensory stage, it is the salient element to which they respond. But it is more than that. Santayana speaks of the beauty of Material in the arts generally as being "the poor man's beauty," inasmuch as no technical knowledge, no erudition, is needed for its enjoyment. It is still more important in that sensitive attention and pleasurable response to Tone is the indispensable prerequisite for all musical development, for it is safe to say that one who has not been led to give sensitive attention and discriminating taste to Tone will take little interest in what tones do in a composition. Finally, it is not only the indispensable basis of musical enjoyment, but it remains, to the end of our lives (even if we become highly-developed musicians), an extremely large factor in our enjoyment.

But before we enlarge on this we must point out a curious oversight in much discussion by aestheticians of the Material of art as appealing to our senses only. For when we have said that Tone appeals to the senses only, we have not said that Tone *only* appeals to the senses. Among aestheticians Louis A. Reid alone, so far as I have read, does full justice to this sense appeal. He points out that even a single tone has form, in that it has definite pitch, length and volume, and that it has quality. Let us add that this same quality is what, for the moment at least, we shall classify as expression—for the tone of a bell, a violin, a trumpet, are surely variously expressive. Sensorial response is therefore not to Tone alone, but to everything the music is doing at a particular moment. This response may grow enormously rich, as when we are addressed by the thrilling sonorities and irridescent colorings of a modern orchestra. Gurney points out that this appeal may be so potent as to quite overwhelm other appeals; as when, at an orchestral concert, we are mentally tired, or are hearing for the first time an elaborate composition, we succumb to the powerful attack upon our senses and catch but the vaguest glimpses of the larger values of Form. Response at that level should not be underestimated. When we have it, which is not infrequently, we have enjoyed an experience that remains in memory as one of quite high value.

The great shortcoming of sensorial response is rather due to its brevity; it cannot relate what engrosses it now to what engrossed it but a moment or two earlier. In music, which exists in time, this momentary nature of sensuous perception has the effect, not experienced in arts that exist in space, of severely contracting the dimensions of that which can be perceived as a unit. Thus, at a suitable distance, the entire stage of a concert hall, with the orchestra seated upon it, would be perceived as a unit. Could our senses attend to it only as they would attend to a musical composition of comparable dimensions, a curtain provided with a window-like aperture would have to be drawn across the stage, revealing a narrow section at a time, and concealing each part as a new part was revealed. Works of architecture, sculpture and painting are thus all before us at once; and if too large for a unitary view, they wait until the eye draws the parts together.

Considering the universality of response to Tone, its basic character, its intensity, and its value, it would appear that to seek beauty and purity of Tone, and develop discrimination with respect to it, in every form of musical activity, should be the paramount concern of every teacher. The task is easier in connection with instrumental music, because in vocal music story-telling or emotionally charged words constantly beckon toward other effects. The glory of our *a cappella* choruses is that they subordinate other possible features of performance to the production of music, often as pure and impersonal as ancient instrumental music. I sometimes think it would be very beneficial if all singers were prohibited from singing any other form of vocal music until they had learned the pure musical possibilities of the voice by some two years' participation in *a cappella* practice. The majestic beauties of Form also come forth in clearer relief when programmatic and highly emotional interests are not advanced to the forefront of attention.

I have been cautious about my use of the word "expression, because Expression as a function of art is the subject of endless debate among aestheticians, and because there is, on the part of laymen (and perhaps particularly with reference to music), such wide diversity of opinion and so much misunderstanding as to what "expression" is and should be. All agree that any work of art seems somehow to be expressive. The difficulty begins when we ask what is expressed. For instance, we may agree that a Greek temple, a Bach fugue, or even (as we cautiously affirmed) the tone of a flute as compared with that of a violin, are variously expressive. But what is expressed? And can such general and unfocused effect rightly be termed expression? Let us dodge long discussion here by following Gurney. No chapter in his widely comprehensive book is more discerning or more powerfully expository than that entitled, "Music as Impressive and Music as Expressive." We can at least agree that all music is at least, in some degree and manner, impressive, and can then examine expression not only as what is supposed to be projected, but also as what we find it to be when we receive it. This two-way view is not only convenient but illuminating.

We may observe, first, that to the layman today and to many eminent musicians, Expression in music connotes emotional expression. That the emotional tone of response to music is more pronounced than that of response to architecture or painting I am not disposed to deny. But there are varieties and grades of feeling, and the word "emotion" connotes to some what Clive Bell disparages as "the emotions of life" as distinguished from "the emotion of beauty"; or what Croce (in his debate with John Dewey in the March 1948 issue of *The Journal of Aesthetics and Art Criticism*) terms "feeling experienced personally" as contrasted to that which "has a universal character." Those two varieties of feeling appear to reflect the two different assumptions (for we can hardly call them consciously adopted beliefs) about the origin and function of music.

The one assumption is that music arose from the "primal cry." You will remember how Wagner, beginning with this premise, ably developed the theory that—curiously enough—made his orchestra the most eloquent and important protagonist in his music dramas. Normally, however, the theory leads one to think of music as being rightly vocal, and unconsciously to assume that instrumental music—all music—strives, or should strive, toward the sort of expression that vocal music, because of its alliance with personal emotional expression, advances prominently to our attention. The words "advances prominently" imply, however, that something else is advanced. That other is the purely musical effects—Tone, with its charm, its energies, its rhythmic appeals, its melodic risings and fallings, the harmonies of the accompaniment. Divested of these—even of the accompaniment alone—the expression of personal emotion would become baldly realistic, and, shorn of other musical graces, could become prosaic and even laughable. Because of their presence, on the other hand, charm remains when song-speech is absent. Wolfram's *Song to the Evening Star*, for instance, played by an orchestra, will charm a hearer who knows nothing of its text or its dramatic role. The impression received is therefore clearly something more than the expression which is assumed to constitute almost all of its value.

The other theory, that music arose from the pleasure of the ear in Tone, suggests that the twang of a bowstring or the long musical tones possible of production by the voice, and used in croonings and calls and wordless melodies—the Swiss yodels are a modern example—were the first musical facts. Now, as W. B. S. Mathews long ago pointed out: "If anyone asserts that the proper function of music is to express emotion of the primal-cry type, or is rather to please the ear as Tone and tonal discourse, no one can successfully contradict him. But, if he asserts that music actually arose in the one way or the other, he has the facts to reckon with." And the facts are that musical instruments were in use quite as early as tribal chants, and that instrumental music has had a much more rapid and extensive development as a form of musical art than has vocal music. But that is because various instruments increase pitch-ranges and tonal colors far beyond the limits possible to human voices, and not because instrumental music is a more natural creation. Nor is there any intimation that instrumental music is superior, as music; the chaste beauty of a few pages by Palestrina may surpass all that a modern orchestra has to say. We merely state that they present for our consideration different types of what is called expression.

The label, "Primal-Cry" connotes an activity of expression; the label, "Pleasure-of-the-Ear-in-Tone," connotes an activity of impression. As we bend our thought specifically on this phase of musical appeal, let us exclude all recognition of non-tonal interests —the story of personal crisis involved in the words of vocal music, or in the program notes of programmatic instrumental music— and ask what music as music, as sheer tones and tonal discourse, can and does express. Immediately, we find ourselves thinking in terms of broad, affective states that we can regard as constituting either the music's expression or our impression—such moods as serenity, tenderness, yearning, tumult, victory, and a thousand others, which no words describe and yet each of which is clearly distinctive and definite.

But is that all? Is the specific affective state not overlaid by, and suffused in, some rare quality of response that is higher, even, than such broad impersonal feeling? Croce's point that "the feeling or sentiment in a work of art is not something experienced personally, but has a universal character" supports our thought to the present point. Projecting it further is Clive Bell's distinction between the "emotions of life" and "the emotion of beauty." I say "projecting it" because it is this last feature of aesthetic experience to which we have come. Or should I say "to which we have ascended?" For no one who has experienced moments of true aesthetic rapture will fail to recognize that to move from the stage of stamping feet and the inarticulate emotional cries of primitive men, to that of programmatic interests, thence to personal emotions, and, still beyond, to the plane where human voices cease and disembodied voices convey some wordless message to us, is to move ever upward.

What then, is this highest message? Why does it so strangely and strongly move us? And to what good? We might say with Santayana that we arrive at "the sense of beauty"—the phrase which he made the title of the book in which he describes the steps of that journey. But the word "beauty" may be debased to connote mere prettiness, and is often inadequate. We would not feel, for instance, that Beethoven's *Ninth Symphony* was described adequately by the word "beautiful." For these and other reasons the idea of beauty has aroused much argument among aestheticians, and the use of the word is deprecated by some. Think how Tolstoi

20 /

spurns it in his book, *What is Art?;* and think, too, of the more virile concept he substitutes. We will do better, I think, to accept Clive Bell's "significant form" as the property that calls forth the highest and purest of aesthetic responses. The question then is what significance the form holds.

An indirect approach may lead us most speedily to the answer to this final question. The cloth woven each day by ordinary life is frayed, fragmentary, pursues no satisfying pattern. To speak in non-figurative language, each day is filled with a welter of little strivings, demands on our attention, frustrations, some satisfactions, some disappointments. It is useless to seek assuagement by making physical life easy and pleasant. Indeed, Clive Bell says that it is "the steady, punctual gnawing of comfort that destroys," and Edna St. Vincent Millay returns this poetic echo to his words, under the title, *Feast.**

> I drank at every vine.
> > The last was like the first.
>
> I came upon no wine
> > So wonderful as thirst.
>
> I gnawed at every root.
> > I ate of every plant.
>
> I came upon no fruit
> > So wonderful as want.
>
> Feed the grape and bean
> > To the vinter and monger;
>
> I will lie down lean
> > With my thirst and my hunger.

What art holds, in contrast to everyday life, is now foreshadowed. With confidence and joy we yield ourselves to the symphony and are borne forth on its current. The journey will not be uneventful, but every question raised will be answered; every tempest encountered won through; every expectation, every yearning, satisfied; and the hunger of the heart for some fair haven that earth seems to deny will be assuaged.

"That earth seems to deny!" In that phrase is implied an answer to my third query, "what value has such experience for humanity?"

---

*From "The Harp-Weaver and Other Poems" by Edna St. Vincent Millay. Harper and Brothers.

It is this: the earth-fettered creature has for a time been emancipated; the disunities and imperfections of life that clouded his vision like a dark mist have been swept away. He cannot live constantly in that clear light; he must return to the duller lustre of daily life. But his eyes have been cleared, his spirit quickened, his faith revived by the revelation that unity and perfection abide in this world, and can be perceived and grasped by man. Pay no heed to those who tell you that this is an escape from life. Life, for each one of us, is his way of beholding it; and this way, compared with other ways, is neither less real nor inferior. Reflect further, that escape must be reckoned in terms not only of what we escape from, but what we escape to, and the spiritual judge within you will surely say that in this case the escape was from a sense of bondage to a sense of high freedom.

Here I should stop. I have defined the goal and its value as well as I am able. But you are in practice, as I once was, and questions of materials and processes are ever before you. For little children not much is needed. Let them hear beauty; in its presence speak softly and with a bit of loving reverence in your voice, so that you will address the intuition and not the eager, acquisitive mind of the children. The mother need not explain the lullaby in a didactic voice; she needs only to sing it tenderly. With older children much—say of motivation, form, expressive features—can be observed, but always with attention to the loveliness so produced, and never as hard facts addressed only to the cognitive mind.

With college groups musical history and biography will help, because they enlarge the conceptual scene in which music is integrated and to every part of which music is related. The danger that they will submerge her voice is not now so great; for the class is now likely to be a selected musical group, and if it is not, the thrusting, cognitive mind has now learned that it cannot elbow its way to the altar. The course may begin indifferently with Palestrina, Shostakovich, France, Germany, Italy, opera, oratorio, song, or symphony, so far as appreciation is concerned. The condition for that is that the study shall not, even for purposes of "full credit," become preponderantly factual. The sky has many constellations. Which is observed first is not so important as that each be observed with full appreciation of its own particular lustre.

THE NEXT ESSAY, "What Is Music For?" was published in the *Music Educators Journal* for June-July 1958. Later on, Mr. Earhart wrote to the editor: "As the time draws near for the publication of my article 'What Is Music For?' as a possible segment of a three-part treatise, I have begun to search my mind and soul for reasons why I should attach such importance to the project. *Was it worthy?* I thought a great deal about it. Then, judging as objectively as I suppose any author can judge his own work, I felt convinced that it was. . . . In this resumé I saw the whole fall into a constant advance toward a goal that I myself had only felt, rather than clearly seen . . . and that goal was higher and greater than had been claimed in the present writings. . . ."

II. WHAT IS MUSIC FOR?

> *The ideas expressed in this paper are equally applicable to all who engage in any activity in the tonal art, from the infant learning to sing, to the solo artist and the conductor of a symphony orchestra. However, music in our public schools has been most specifically in our thought. There are two reasons for this: the article had its origin in connection with a problem in music education, and secondly, and of more importance, music and art in our public schools are supported by taxes levied upon all our people, and constitute by far the largest subsidy given the fine arts by our government.*
>
> *In contrast, almost all other activities in music, such as private teaching and the work of privately owned music schools, represent dealings between individuals, and the outside public does not concern itself with the cost, efficiency, policies or values to human life of the transactions. Nor do the musicians involved need to know what values are being contributed.*
>
> *But service to the whole nation, the value of which the public has often questioned, and the nature of which is often not clear even to boards of education and superintendents of schools—yes, and to supervisors and teachers of music themselves—certainly needs to be understood and appreciated.*
>
> *And who but those who teach, or who influence the teaching of music in our public schools should lead the way? It might be a good policy if all engaged in any form of activity in the tonal art followed their example.*
> —W.E.

IN A LETTER received before this paper was undertaken, my respected colleague, Karl Gehrkens, quoted from Will Durant's book, *Mansions of Philosophy*, a definition of philosophy that captured my thought. Shortly afterward, in a conversation, A. Verne Wilson deplored those college courses which, although designed to train public school music teachers and supervisors, fail to inspire in the future teachers a feeling of dedication to a high mission—this, no doubt, because the instructors themselves had not been enlightened, or because they could not impart their knowledge and sense of dedication to their students. My friend Wilson deplored this the more since the necessary stress in education on science and technology requires constant restatement of and emphasis on spiritual values.

Let us look at these views, which are also those of this author, in the light of Will Durant's definition:

"Technically, as we defined it long ago, philosophy is 'a study of experience as a whole, or of a portion of experience in relation to the whole.' At once it becomes clear that any problem can be the material of philosophy, if only it is studied in total perspective, in the light of all human experience and desire."

The failure, then, so far as there is failure in teaching music education, is in teaching that subject in a vacuum, in not connecting and coordinating it with all other areas of human interest and experience—all of which means having no philosophy of the subject. It is obvious that anything and everything about music and the teaching of music, studied in such isolation without giving the one spark that would irradiate the whole, namely, an understanding of what it is all about or why it is done at all, is a lamentable dereliction. Only the deep aesthetic "resonance" as Jacob Kwalwasser felicitously termed it, gives to some teaching an inspirational quality; but fine as this is, it is not enough unless accompanied by a clear understanding of the values of such aesthetic experience. Without that clear understanding and philosophical knowledge the aesthetically sensitive teacher has no defense against the common view that it is all a matter of taste and inborn proclivities—just as one becomes a wizard at sharp-shooting or playing chess.

One phase of music must, however, be discussed in separation from the whole of man's concept of life; and that is the nature of music itself. In these days, when radio networks blandly announce long periods of "music" (sic); by famous (sic) bands and singers (sic); and the listener hears demented melodies wandering around aimlessly looking for, but never finding, some solid place to light; strange cacophonies played by strange, shrill, strident instruments from which the players seem to try to extract the worst possible quality of tone, playing in jerking, spasmodic, hiccoughing rhythm

—held together only by a steady machine-like chug-chug, chug-chug of a bass instrument; with crooners singing silly words—pardon, lyrics—that a child of ten years should be ashamed of, in dementia praecox style—when all this and other sounds and noises are called "music" (the same name given to what the civilized world formerly knew as music), *it then becomes necessary to describe music as it is conceived in this article.*

Such vagaries of rhythm and sound, together with their attendant bodily abandon, led this author in earlier writings to call it a neural spree and abdication of the central government. Developments since have made those terms even more truly descriptive.

Meanwhile we proclaim ever more seriously the dignity of man. But George Washington danced to the music of the stately minuet, as contrasted to rock and roll. If we look too fixedly and long upon this passing psychosis we may be tempted to say with Elijah, in Mendelssohn's oratorio of that name: "It is enough, O Lord. Now take away my life, for I am not better than my fathers."

Let us then, at least as a working hypothesis, state the properties that are essential to real music. They are three:

1. Every tone, vocal or instrumental, should be as pure, as pleasing, as lovely, as possible.

2. In combination the tones should respect the physical laws of acoustics, and of aural reception which reflects those laws, and be fairly concordant—not wholly cacophonous.

3. There should be, as in any product addressed to other than infantile intelligence, some recognizable form or design.

The inclusion of cacophonous music in Item 2 was made reluctantly, chiefly to pay tribute to many modern compositions that are strong, worthy and often deeply impressive, and secondly to point out that *beautiful* and *impressive* are not synonymous terms, although the two qualities may exist concurrently. This is because it is impossible to account for our sense of beauty except as an impression. On the other hand, all sorts of sounds—single tones and combinations of tones—may be *impressive;* may indeed be frightening, exciting, startling, awesome, or just downright disagreeable, and destitute of beauty. Much of modern music—and indeed of all the fine arts—appears to aim at impressiveness, and presents beauty only incidentally or almost accidentally.

The only basis for argument between the protagonists for impressiveness at whatever loss of beauty, and those who hold beauty as pre-eminent, is: *which is the natural and rightful function of the fine arts?*

History records that beauty is cherished and admired for centuries after the unbeautiful impressive works of man have been forgotten. One must say, however, that a totally unbeautiful impressive quality may have useful artistic value, especially as used in opera and drama. We believe, however, that an impression of beauty contributes a higher value to mankind than an impression of awesome grandeur or power. The feeling produced by the appearance of shimmering rainbows in the mists arising from Niagara Falls elevates and purifies man's spirit more than does the impression of the tremendous power of the cataract. Beethoven appears to be the classical composer who at times most nearly gives us both; Mozart the one who gives us most consistently pure musical beauty. He expressed that feeling when, in a letter to his father, he wrote that even in the most tragic situations in opera, music should still be pleasing to the ear.

This confusion between all sorts of impressiveness in modern compositions and sheer musical beauty leads to the equating of two qualities of essentially different nature. The inequality of the two values in our musical progress is also greatly increased when we consider the number of people participating in musical activities. In public education alone, millions make progress in music without coming into any significant contact with Stravinsky, Schoenberg, Bartok or others of the modern school. Under private teachers of voice, piano, violin and other instruments, uncounted thousands also make no contact. Composers, conductors of opera and symphony orchestras and their audiences constitute, as they did with Wagner, the larger part of those who engage in the valuable task of introducing this new cacophonous musical language to the world.

If the reader will for the present accept this concept of music, we can proceed to discuss the philosophy of music—that is, music in its relation to the whole of man's experience, and its value as compared with the values of other areas of experience. Only when that is done successfully and convincingly can the question "What is Music For?"

be answered. There is no need for long and abstruse philosophic reflection or aesthetic discussion; a little common-sense reflection on one's own experience should be sufficient.

Perhaps we should start with the broadest possible generalization about man's areas of interest and attention, and divide them into two broad categories, which we will term *otherness* and *selfness*. This could be reduced or sharpened further by William Tomlin's statement of theosophic origin: "We live within three concentric circles: self-regarding, others-regarding, and God-regarding." If, instead of *others* we substitute *other fields of attention, personal and impersonal,* we can include, as does Max Schoen, the selfless dedication of the scientist in seeking the ultimate physical facts that govern the material cosmos and the areas of religious and aesthetic absorption.

Repeating the general thought of selfless areas of interest is another quotation:

>Threefold is the search for perfection
>   That runs through creation's plan,
>Through immemorial nature
>   And the restless heart of man;
>Beauty of form and color
>   To gladden the heart and eye,
>Truth without cavil or question
>   To answer the reason why;
>And the blameless spirit's portion
>   The joy that shall not die.

And so music, together with all the fine arts, and beauty in nature —and to some degree in almost every product of man's fashioning— satisfies a hunger in the heart of man and gives him delight quite apart from any material gain or advantage it can bring to him. Thus his chairs could be as comfortable and as sturdy without grace of design, his pottery as useful without adornment and glaze; but they would then bring satisfaction only to the most primitive man —if even to him—for all primitive peoples have sought to add adornment to their products.

While utilitarian objects may be beautiful, beauty itself is not utilitarian. True, a symphony may be sold to a publisher, and usually the price paid is in inverse ratio to the beauty or merit of the composition. The musicians and conductor who perform it are paid for that service, usually in the same ratio. The money so received may then be spent—indeed, for the most part, *must* be spent—for food, clothing, shelter, furniture, or other prosaic, useful things; meanwhile, composition and performance remain things of beauty that have no such use. *What, then, is music for?*

Changing to another art, namely, drama, we have Aristotle's famous doctrine of catharsis; by arousing in us the emotions of pity and fear, it purges and cleanses the soul. It is to the credit of human beings that the question *purges of what?* is so seldom asked. Instinctively we know that it is of some lower, baser content—the little cares and plans and strivings that must be managed to the advantage of ourselves, or at least without detriment to our affairs or to our reputation. In short, we are released from the plane of littleness and selfness, and find ourselves purified and elevated. We do not need philosophers and aestheticians to tell us this. Even a rainbow, or a starry sky, may make the fussy, disturbing world drop away for some moments and leave us in a tranquil, a far-seeing mood.

Or you may leave the concert hall with the spell of the orchestra still upon you and step out on the clanging street; and the spell is broken, the world of selfness returns. You must hurry home. That night letter must be dispatched to your business colleague telling him the hour of your arrival, and your bags are not yet fully packed. There is a feeling of a return to a lower plane of living, but that plane is not so low as it would have been had not the spell of the concert overflowed into it. We cannot live on that high plane forever, but those blessed detached moments melt into the whole of experience.

It would be a pity if music had no life after the performers had left and gone their separate ways, and the concert hall was dark and silent. Yet if the composition is one being given its premiere we know its life is just beginning, and if old the performance is a renewed birth in the minds and hearts of the performers and all who heard it. Memories of the moods and excitements it created come back to cast their spell for days, perhaps to the end of one's life.

Max Schoen first called my attention to Edna St. Vincent Millay's poem, *The Concert,* in much the same connection that our thought now pursues. Incidentally, it is a superb example of the right way to listen to music. In a beautiful metaphor she hears the music as Bach must have heard his fugues, namely, the engrossing adventures of tones without thought of relation to human beings or to human life. Only a few lines of the poem are quoted here, and these are not in their original order:

>   Armies clean of love and hate
>   . . . Hurling terrible javelins down
>   From the shouting walls of a singing town
>   Where no women wait!
>   No, I will go alone . . .
>   I will come back to you . . .
>   And you will know me still.
>   I shall be only a little taller
>   Than when I went.*

"Taller than when I went"—no words could better express the elevation and purification of mood that follows such aesthetic experience; in this case an experience produced by giving one's self to following the adventures of Tone. What else calls forth the strong and fluctuating feelings with which we follow a Bach fugue through its mounting progress to a triumphant conclusion? And even in monophonic music and in vocal music for solo or chorus, with its words, we are affected chiefly, although unconsciously, by what we are here calling the adventures of Tones. If those are rather poor misadventures we say, perceivingly, that it is "a very poor tune."

It cannot be said too often or too emphatically, especially to teachers of music in public schools, that Tone is the stuff of which music is made, that a single tone may be beautiful as a single flower is beautiful; and that the desire and effort to produce it in itself promotes aesthetic development. Such development may begin in the kindergarten, attend the "curing" of monotones, and banish embarrassment in teaching the boy whose voice is changing the techniques by which he may again assist in making music.

---

* From "The Harp-Weaver and Other Poems" by Edna St. Vincent Milllay. Harper and Brothers. The complete poem, "The Concert," appears on page 95.

Although we may not realize it, the adventures of Tone fascinate us. They are of infinite variety, and no two compositions among the millions that exist are alike. If we think of the range in voices from soprano to bass, of instruments from piccolo to bass viol—of the tone color of these, in chord structures, modes and speeds of motion, the infinite number of possibilities is apparent. Nor do we need the resources of great symphonic works to give us variety. A simple solo with piano accompaniment, and in spite of its words—yes, even without accompaniment, say the "Londonderry Air"—rings in our memory as a tonal excursion, and its charm and worth are assessed as such. No words would save it if the tune were extremely poor.

Obviously there are all degrees of aesthetic experience, due not only to the degree of richness of the aesthetic subject, but also to the sensitivity of those sharing the experience. Age is also a factor in this aspect of the discussion. The infant in the cradle is obviously pleased and soothed by soft sweet sounds and fretted by loud, angry voices or clattering, smashing sounds. Later, his speech and his singing voice will improve, and his tastes and sensitivity to tonal communication will be the better if early preferences are noted and used to direct his course. But such matters, though powerfully influential to the infant, are of small moment to youths or adults, with their longer attention span and memory, and therefore their power to integrate longer successions of tones into a single unit. This does not mean, however, that the infant should not *hear* long compositions, but only that he should not be expected to have specific responses to them. God shows the infant as large a sky as the adult sees, but the infant is not expected to make specific astronomical observations. One should remember, however, that the infant is closer to Mozart than to Tchaikowsky or Berlioz.

Aesthetic experiences differ in kind as well as in degree. Beauties that are seen differ from those that are heard. This springs from the diverse nature and functions of the sense organs employed. Sight is a "long-distance notifier," hearing, a "short-distance notifier"— and this implies that sound strikes closer home, so to speak. In primitive life, sound was the stronger signal to quickened action and aroused more emotion, while sight aroused comparatively more deliberate and calm appraisal. Another difference is that sounds die immediately they are made, while a painting, however large, remains motionless, or a landscape remains immovable until the eye can move over it again and again, until the areas of the scene become fused in the mental picture.

The immediate appeal of sound to the feelings, together with no demand to hold and appraise the continuous flow must, one must think, be the cause of its appeal to a much wider public—and we are speaking still of music as we defined it, and not of other sounds. These matters are mentioned here only because they bear on the type of musical experience appropriate to children and others of various ages.

Little that has been said in this paper is new. Many music teachers have been aware for years, consciously or otherwise, of the significance of beauty in their work. But if the value of beauty in music is so great, it deserves an almost religious dedication on the part of music teachers; their job must encompass more than the technical aspects of music, with no truckling to popularity.

Two more comments may be pertinent.

Just as the selfless nature of science in its search for ultimate physical truths may become suspect because its discoveries may so often lead to technological production of utilitarian things of doubtful or even of evil character, so may the true function of beauty be obscured when it is lavished on poor or even evil things. Thus a tavern may be made more beautiful than a church. But no lover of truth buys the utilitarian article to satisfy his hunger for truth, and no lover of beauty goes to the tavern to satisfy his hunger for beauty. The practical person and the lover of beauty recognize that both science and adornment have been transplanted to a foreign soil in which they were not and never would become rooted.

We have used the words "as beautiful as possible" in connection with all attempts to produce beauty. The *possible* in that connection was the limit of capability of the producer. If, however, we think of the word "possible" as applied to conception, we extend possibilities limitlessly. The search then is for perfection—a far-off, vague concept, which would not be recognizable even were human beings able to attain it. This is the search in which the great minds in history have engaged—a search that has no sure or recognizable end. Einstein in science; Michelangelo in art; Beethoven, as his notebooks show, striving to perfect many of his compositions; Toscanini striving endlessly to perfect his performance of Beethoven's *Ninth Symphony* before he would let it be recorded. But for us, infinitely more humble workers, their example is a good one to follow, for it tells us not to think of what *we* can *do,* but of what it, the work, *demands.* Whether we approach the goal nearly or only remotely is not the question. We shall be in the service of Perfection, and there is no greater or more rewarding service.

This writing is finished at a time when the United States is almost frantically calling for a gigantic increase in a type of education that would make us equal or superior to the Russians in what is the characteristic and outstanding feature of their culture. This is not, one may assume, because we repudiate the type of culture that our country has developed, and which has given Americans so much of physical ease and comfort, and wide areas of cultural interests and high spiritual values such as the Russians still do not have— although unquestionably they have the capacity to enjoy. We do not wish to substitute the Russian culture for our own, and it may be well for us to learn that we have been too soft with our children at all levels, from the elementary school to and through our high schools and universities. It would be a sad day, however, if, in the effort to add strength and toughness to one phase of our culture, we should lose the amplitude and richness of interests and the wide dissemination of knowledge and culture that now characterizes this land of ours. We can and must support this new effort, and still maintain the many priceless values we have won.

... "IT REMAINS TO OBSERVE", says the author in the next and final article of this section (Part III of Section One) "that man's non-utilitarian areas of interest, although they do not claim so many hours of his attention, are as numerous and as diverse in kind as his practical interests. Also, there is a hierarchy of values among the non-utilitarian fields of attention just as there is a hierarchy of values among the many ways in which man works to earn a livelihood. The two fields are not similar, however, in this respect; even the lowest place in the non-utilitarian category is not without honor, while in the practical field a man's way of gaining a living might be too base or criminal to mention. On that basis the whole hierarchy appears to divide itself into two classes, one of the highest nobility, the other of only lesser nobility . . ."

III. CONGENITAL AND CHANGING ACQUIRED INTERESTS

> *In this essay the area is broadened to include all the experiences of man, and these are now discussed as to their relative spiritual and idealistic value.* —W.E.

THE NEED FOR SUCH a discussion as this arises from the fact that few people realize the value to mankind of preoccupation with the non-utilitarian interests, or how much attention almost everyone gives daily to such interests.

It seems strange that this is true, in face of the fact that all sorts of concerts and art exhibits are attended, and people travel the world over to see things of beauty. There are a number of ways in which we escape from the commonplace, worldly interests. They vary in length, in frequency, in continuity, and in intensity. None of these characteristics becomes a measure of value; the experience may be longer but shallow, or short but intense. We may, however, distinguish the categories in all such experiences.

The first category is wholly removed from any conceivable concern with the worldly things of life. At the head of this category would be the religious recluse or the missionary, who feels that he is in direct communication with God.

Why, then, the need for a rational analysis of the nature and value of preoccupation with non-utilitarian interests?

The answer is to be found in the outlook of man upon his world. In medieval times that world was a work of God, to the glory of Whom they erected upflung Gothic cathedrals, which reverence demanded should be, even to the smallest detail, of the most chaste and pure beauty that the humble workers could conceive. It was a finished world to be accepted as it was; and being ruled by heavenly powers, man should not rebel against climatic rigors, catastrophies or conditions of living.

The Renaissance not only brought a great revival in learning and the arts but witnessed events that changed profoundly during three centuries the outlook of man upon his world. The discoveries of Columbus and other great voyagers thrilled all mankind with visions of a new world larger than that which was known to them, and not finished but inviting settlement where better living conditions existed or could be created by bringing natural conditions under control. Then, in the telling phrase of Jung, "the vertical outlook of the European mind was forthwith intersected by the horizontal outlook of modern times."

Then were sown the first seeds of natural science with its attendant technologies, seeds that produced a growth of such gigantic proportions that the whole world marveled at its achievements. Today this natural science, the "science of matter," to use Henri Bergson's phrase, is frantically trying to outdo the wholly materialistic efforts of the Russians. Today natural science absorbs more of the attention and activity of mankind than ever before.

The new outlook, however, produced social changes that are of vastly more significance than its material products. It led to the industrial revolution, which substituted machine-tenders for craftsmen, divided man into classes under the labels of capital and labor, which in turn led to Marxian communism. Nor did it stop there. Its philosophy, as formulated by Francis Bacon, who states plainly that it applies only to matter known to the physical senses, and not to "the divine"—that is, to spiritual or metaphysical areas of man's life—came to be regarded by many as a philosophy that was applicable to all of man's life. Thus arose the dichotomy of science vs. religion. Science also turned its outlook upon education. Thus the I.Q. was measured, tests and measurements became an organized department in educational annual reports.

Except for communism, none of these outcomes of the new outlook is set down in deprecation. They are reported only to emphasize the inability of science to see, describe or advise man except as to his physical being. Natural science demands precision, and precision must be made in units of measurement. Abstract qualities —love, beauty, holiness, perseverance, faith, hope, charity—these can be roughly reckoned by actions that can be seen, but they have no units of measurement such as degrees of temperature or inches or miles of space, pounds, decibels and megatons and what not. Nevertheless, science has been so powerful in shaping our world anew that nothing is quite important and believable unless it has been scientifically proven to be so.

So we return to the question which set off this long retrospect: "Why do we need rational analysis of the nature and value of preoccupation with non-utilitarian interests" when such preoccupation is experienced in some way and degree by every individual, and is consequently so sympathetically supported? The obvious answer is that scientific methods have so dominated the thought and activities of all mankind that every conclusion or belief, however widely held in the intuitions of man, is considered by many as being false or at least untrustworthy unless and until it is "proven" by scientific methods. This, however, poses a quandary; for the "sciences of matter" cannot deal with the incorporeal (or metaphysical or spiritual) such as the value of preoccupation with non-utilitarian interests.

The case is not lost, however, for there are other ways in which rational proof can be given. As an instance, many believe now that economic inflation can be halted, even permanently prevented. An exhaustive study of history by Arnold Toynbee has, on the contrary, led him to state that every nation that has had a coinage has experienced a continuing depreciation in the value of that coinage. Similarly, we can see what benefits science and technology have given to man, and compare these as given to different nations. In the same way we can see what the value we are now seeking to prove has brought to different countries in the degree of culture attained, and the honor accorded them by other countries. We could cite Germany before the first world war in the first case, and ancient Greece in the second. On the whole the culture of a people is remembered and honored more than the material prosperity and power that a people may attain. Moreover, each individual man knows which of his activities have blest him and which have been empty of value or may even have left him with a bad conscience, and this, too, is history—the history of an individual's mind.

It remains to observe that man's non-utilitarian areas of interest, although they do not claim so many hours of his attention, are as numerous and as diverse in kind as his practical interests. Also, there is a hierarchy of values among the non-utilitarian fields of attention just as there is a hierarchy of values among the many ways in which man works to earn a livelihood. The two fields are not similar, however, in this respect: even the lowest place in the non-utilitarian category is not without honor, while in the practical field a man's way of gaining a living might be too base or criminal to mention. On that basis the whole hierarchy appears to divide itself into two classes, one of the highest nobility, the other of only lesser nobility. Each class doubtless contains many subdivisions, but even to attempt to name all of them would be a work of supererogation.

The validity of the rankings accorded in a hierarchy of values can be attested only in terms of the esteem in which each individual holds the particular experience, and, much more importantly, the esteem with which mankind as a whole has come to regard them. The value grows in proportion to the remoteness which the subject has from practical earthly living.

According to the foregoing criterion, the highest of all values to man would be preoccupation with religious adoration, with the feeling of direct communion with God. In this the spirit is purified and elevated to a realm beyond the clamor of earthly life. When the hours of such communion are ended and the participant returns to the ordinary tasks of life, that spirit remains to bless all later hours, and all men have come to recognize the value of that spirit.

Perhaps the second item in this regal category is preoccupation with beauty in its many forms. All men seek beauty; all men have always honored the artist. No nation is honored if it produces nothing but utilitarian products, and if that production is great the nation is rather feared or envied. Man does not live by bread alone or for bread alone, for his mind and spirit too have their hungers.

A second category might well be described as preoccupation with humanitarian ideals and sympathies. At the head would be the religious missionary who often risks, and has often lost, his life in a passionate desire to lead a tribe into such a nearness to God as has blest his own life. A missionary of this kind also ranks at the head of the preceding category.

Within the numerous and very large groups engaged in humanitarian activities are some members—but not all—who are wholly preoccupied with non-utilitarian interests: the Red Cross, the Y.M.C.A. and Y.W.C.A., the Community Chest or United Fund, CARE, nurses in hospitals, rest homes or other locations. Army surgeons are typical of this class.

The distinction made above, "some members—but not all," has been long overdue, for it applies to the "regal" category quite as well as to the one now being discussed. Persons of small intellect, little knowledge, vulgar interests, questionable motives, or all of these, may invade occasionally the most exalted plane of man's activities and degrade it. Thus we may have quack preachers who from pulpit, tent or street corner harangue people into false conceptions of the nature of religion and the love of God, quack musicians who dishonor music and confuse a public when their crude sensationalism brings them into prominence which seems to make them popular, and their accumulation of wealth, that greatly exceeds that of Bach, Mozart, Handel, Beethoven and Brahms combined, seems to make them greatly approved by the world.

These observations are made in order to guard us from the assumption that preoccupation with an interest of man cannot be assessed by the rank accorded that interest, but only by the elevation of mind with which an individual approaches it. Thus a comparatively lowly interest may be blest by a lofty outlook upon it, just as a comparatively lofty area may be degraded by a debased outlook upon it. This observation further applies to all areas of interest that might be explored in such an inquiry as this. The ensuing paragraphs touch briefly upon some of these other areas of interest, but, for reasons mentioned, deal specifically with music and music education only.

The first category, however, has no possible relation to standards of living and improvement in worldly conditions, and it is noticeable that the more purely idealistic the interest, the more the experience elevates the spirit.

The overall purpose of this essay, indeed, is to attribute the dignity of man as due to the possession of spiritual and idealistic elements not possessed by any other animate creature yet known to man; to point out the fact that this dignity has been obscured in recent decades as by a miasmatic fog, by the horrible, savage and ruthless torture and massacre of uncounted millions of men, women and children; and to urge that we regain some of the respect for ourselves that we may have lost, and give these elements greater place in our endeavors.

Metaphorically speaking, these are the only travelers we can send into orbit in outer space, where they gather and transmit and bring back to earth visions and understandings not so clearly seen in the murkier atmosphere of earth, and where they become the treasured legacy that forms the basis of our highest civilization and culture. It is to this end and in that faith that all the preceding pages have been written.

♦

Will Earhart's original manuscript ended here. Although printed just as submitted for publication, there are various evidences that Mr. Earhart had hoped—possibly expected—to add more by way of extension, expansion, illumination or elucidation of certain points covered in the three parts indicated as Section One of this book. Whether this was his purpose is not clear; in any event the contents of Section Two, taken from Mr. Earhart's previous writings, do without question well serve various of the ends enumerated.

—C.V.B.

SECTION TWO

WILL EARHART, TEACHER, PHILOSOPHER

A selection of papers,
addresses, and other
writings published from
1914 through 1938.

A QUEST FOR BASIC PRINCIPLES

> *The full title of this paper, presented at the 1926 meeting of the Music Supervisors National Conference at Detroit, Michigan, was "Music and Its Function: A Quest for Basic Principles." The 1926 Detroit convention is notable in MENC history for the first National High School Orchestra, forerunner of important if not to say major, developments in music education.*

THE ESSENTIAL NATURE of our modern occidental civilization is due to the place held by science and the application of science to industry. The effect of scientific thought and action is to make vast changes in the material world surrounding us. We dredge, build, transform and transport matter to an extent never before attempted or sought. By this action we seek—and attain, until the action is overdone—material comfort and well-being.

Science is characteristically quantitative. It proceeds out of the rational intellect. Henri Bergson, in *Creative Evolution,* says: "The rational intellect is formed on matter and its purpose is the manipulation of matter." The aspect of the world about us proves the point. Before the rise of science, life was, proportionately, more subjective. It probably was not absolutely more subjective; but the amount of effort given to the transformation of matter, to the manipulation of our material environment, was relatively so much less that the greater emphasis of thought was upon the living of human life as subjectively experienced.

In England that stage of development flowered in the Elizabethan poets; in other countries and periods it gave birth to periods of philosophical and religious thought and periods of art-development of all kinds. I do not mean that religion, philosophy or art has ever been restricted to such periods: I mean that it has characterized them, just as material production characterizes the occidental civilization of our period.

Undoubtedly we derive certain satisfactions from the production, acquisition, and use of things—even some of the myriads of things that shriek at us from blazing electric signs and that clutter up our homes—but it is idle to suppose that we will have satisfied all the desires and aspirations of our hearts when we have arrived at a hypothetical saturation point in material progress. There is no such saturation point. Instead, desires grow with exercise. As well might we expect to make the infant happy by filling his nursery with ever more and more costly toys.

The scientific, quantitative measure is the one characteristically applied to life today. Because of the nature and field of action of the rational intellect it will measure life in objective terms, or in terms of advance in power to conquer the material world.

But in *Education and the Larger Life,* by C. Hanford Henderson, is a statement that I never tire of repeating, and which many of you must have heard me use. It is this: "If man is the highest product of creation, then civilization must be judged not by what man produces but by the manner of man produced." A simple criterion, is it not? And no more to be gainsaid than a Euclidian axiom: yet it turns our attention from the objective to the subjective: it envisions man as the product and the things about him, upon which he acts, as valuable only in terms of their reaction upon him. Possessing it, we no longer measure our status by tonnage, bricks, stones, and steel, and the knowledge that gives power to deal with these things, but by the physical, mental, moral and spiritual strength of the human beings around us. We *do* more today, we *have* more; but *are* we more? If we glance back at our ancestors do we see that our fathers and mothers were somewhat poor creatures compared with ourselves, and that their parents were still more dwarfed in physical, mental and spiritual stature? Once upon a time, Elijah swept such a glance back, and cried out in bitter anguish: "It is enough, Oh Lord! Now take away my life, for am I not better than my fathers."

Education, because educators have not yet issued their declaration of independence and assumed their highest position of leadership, has come to reflect largely the view of life current in the world outside; although there it flourishes among persons whose philosophical depth is hardly sufficient to entitle them to such a position as educational leaders. The child is envisioned as an instrument that is to be sharpened so that it may cut as deeply as possible into life. What the individual will do, will produce in life, is a concern that is reflected in a great many of our latest educational processes and lines of thought. What life will do in and to the individual, envisioning him as the product, receives less emphasis. We might well heed more these words of Ruskin:

An education "which shall keep a good coat on my son's back; which shall enable him to ring with confidence the visitors' bell at double-belled doors; which shall result ultimately in establishment of a double-belled door to his own house—in a word, which shall lead to advancement in life—this we pray for on bent knees; and this is all we pray for." It never seems to occur to the parents that there may be an education which, in itself, is advancement in Life— that any other than that may perhaps be advancement in Death; and that this essential education may be more easily got, or given, than they fancy, if they set about it in the right way; while it is for no price, and by no favor, to be got, if they set about it in the wrong.

Since our occidental world-scheme is based on science, and is characteristically quantitative, it is inevitable that education, as far as it follows the prevailing mode, will base its program on the scientific outlook and will think of educational progress, both in general and in the individual, in quantitative terms—and since this outlook has arisen because the shrewd, planning intellect, rather than the humble, questioning, aspiring soul, has been accepted as our true prophet, the psychology of education, in so far as education follows the prevailing mode, will be cognitive or thinking psychology rather than a psychology of the feelings, the emotions. Indeed, psychology itself, as distinguished from its nearest prototype, philosophy, is a product of the scientific age: and it is notable, that accordingly we have a large and confident rational psychology but only a meagre—though not correspondingly humble—psychology of feeling.

For our purposes—meaning by "our" the purposes of most of those who are gathered here—we need a profound and discerning psychology and philosophy of feeling; and that psychology should not, following the current illusion that only objective knowledge is real, express itself in terms of physiological reactions, but should express itself in terms of subjective experience. This is because the scientific study of the physiological reactions connected with emotion will not be sufficiently refined and complete to discover and explain the infinite variety of general states of feeling that account for personality, or the numberless delicate grades and shades of feeling that characterize such affective states as our various aesthetic reactions. It may note physiological changes in connection with the violent reactions to circumstance within the familiar psychological trinity, fight, flight and love; but I doubt its efficacy in discovering what happens to my fleshly counterpart when I gaze on a rainbow as compared with what happens when I hear a Beethoven symphony. Besides, it doesn't matter. What happens to me is more important than what happens to some of my glands and in my blood stream. James says something to the effect that when we have traced the flow of some magnetic current along some gray fibre and have witnessed some molecular changes in some gray matter within the skull, we have nowhere lighted on the poet's dream. Strange that we should search for it there! Or, that searching and not finding, we should, in another dream, deny the existence of the first dream.

So far we have been assembling certain "properties" without which our performance could not go forward. We may now begin to use them.

All art—and music certainly not less than other arts—primarily differs in outlook and method from that science which today assumes to settle all questions, in that it arises from, and addresses itself to, certain states of sympathy or feeling, instead of arising from and addressing the cognitive faculties. Bergson, in *Creative Evolution*, points out that rational intellect—meaning pure intellect—can see in a human face only an assemblage of features, but that it is exactly behind this appearance that the artist, by an act that Bergson calls "divining sympathy," so places himself that he may discern the intention that runs through and unifies the lines into a purposeful face.

Bergson defines this intuitional, impulsive, willing, moving force as life itself, and describes the rational intellect as never able to comprehend it; as "awkward in the presence of life itself," to use his own words; and as standing outside of life and taking snapshots of it from various angles, but never entering into it. If I may interpret by a figure, we may say that the divining, feeling, moving force is as the seeing eye, while the rational intellect is as a different optical apparatus, which can examine the seeing eye but never quite join with it in its visions. The divining, feeling, moving force can be comprehended only by a like divining, feeling force. It cannot itself see; nor can the intellect that runs by its side truly know it.

If we accept this account we shall see that art differs from science not only in resting upon feeling instead of cognition, but also in the fact that it is essentially subjective and concerns itself with inward qualities rather than with objective quantities.

Now I take it for granted that we who teach music are all more concerned with what music can do in the individual than with what the individual can do in music. It is true that the individual must do something in music before music can do something in him; but since we are concerned primarily with the quality of subjective reaction, it ill behooves us to adopt the scientific mode of measuring results quantitatively, until we have first made sure that the type of action we prescribe is one that will react upon the individual in the highest and most beneficent terms. Any sort of music, taught in any way, from any angle of approach, to any persons at any time, may fail pitiably in exerting that regenerative power which I believe it is the mission of art to wield. James Russell Lowell has stated it for me. (Parenthetically, this reminds me of the plaint of Mark Twain, that "the ancients had stolen all of his best thoughts.") I take the Lowell quotation from Neuhaus's book, *The Appreciation of Art*.

"Till America has learned to love art, not as an amusement, not as a mere ornament of her cities, not as a superstition of what is *comme il faut* for a great nation, but for humanizing and ennobling energy, for its power of making men better by arousing in them a perception of their own instinct for what is beautiful, and therefore sacred and religious and an eternal rebuke of the base and worldly, she will not have succeeded in that high sense which alone makes a nation out of a people, and raises it from a dead name to a living power."

Accepting this statement of the mission of art, what, then, is the essential factor in musical art, which, if we discover and use it, will advance us toward the fulfillment of that mission? Ordinarily the central factor in music is thought of as emotion; and a peculiar and limited connotation is attached to the word "emotion." Because the thought, so limited, constitutes a lamentably incomplete and misleading aesthetic doctrine, we will center our discussion of the essential nature of music around it.

Ribot, in his book, *Diseases of Personality*, states that the sense, conscious or subconscious, of the condition of the skin, viscera, bodily organs, etc., constitutes for each and every one of us his personality. I do not endorse that materialistic point of view: but I cite his point of view for the purpose of calling your attention to the reality of broad, general states of feeling—we will call them affective states—that are quite different from those sharp, emotional reactions to specific conditions or stimuli which we ordinarily connote when we use the word "emotions." Clive Bell, in his book *Art*—another book which I am continually citing—has a similar distinction in mind when he sharply contrasts what he terms "the emotion of beauty." Ethel Puffer, whose account, by the way, is much the most absorbing and masterly that I have read, in her book *The Psychology of Beauty*, proceeds in like vein to discuss the specific "emotions" that have come to be associated with musical experience, as quite different from that genuine aesthetic reaction which she evidently believes it is the real purpose of music to evoke.

The general affective state is described in the report of the Music Committee of the Commission on the Curriculum, published in the Fourth Yearbook, 1926, of the Department of Superintendence of the National Education Association,* as "the particular complex of emotional forces of an individual in a state of balance." On the other hand, to quote further: "Emotions of the specific kind represent increased emotional energy attained by stimulation that overturns, for a time, this state of balance in favor of driving energies of a particular kind." The report continues: "By the same terms, aesthetic feeling may be described as increased emotional energy without loss of balance; and this is a condition of heightened power, expanded and quickened sense of life and general well-being, happily devoid of those less well balanced and perhaps even violent impulses that may characterize specific emotions."

The specific emotions, well named by Clive Bell "the emotions of life," take their rise from situations in life that are fraught with dramatic or emotional possibilities, and these situations and emotions we follow in imagination and in full sympathy. They are not intrinsic in music itself, for music is tone and tonal design or procedure. They constitute an associated and extrinsic interest,

---

* Now named the American Association of School Administrators, A Department of the National Education Association of the United States. (NEA Building, 1201 Sixteenth Street N.W., Washington 6, D. C.)

aroused by words or programs—or even by our own imaginations—if we are fettered to the realities of human life and are unable or unready to soar into an idealistic realm on "wings of music." They are not incompatible with music, but they are not music and neither represent the essential purpose of music or become a proper criterion of its value—as any composer (born before 1895) will tell you. In so far as any such interests are associated with music they give us a hybrid art. This is not to say that the product is a lesser art, but merely to say that it is not a purely musical art. Wagner saw this very clearly, and considered himself the creator of a new art rather than a composer pure and simple.

The emotion or affective state created in us by music itself differs in an extraordinary degree, in both character and genesis, from the emotions aroused by associated interests. In so far as we experience it, it is generated by the tones themselves. They speak in beauty, enthralling our attention by their loveliness as sound alone. They rise and fall, they shout and whisper, they run or creep despondently, they build up architectural glories that are divinely alluring, and that almost cause us to catch our breath, because they fade even as they are born. By reason of the beautiful relationships that exist between them, the tones call to one another across the pages. They clamor, question and entreat and at last shout triumphantly their mutual understanding. All this is done in balance and symmetry. Every expectation aroused is bountifully fulfilled, every stress is healed. All this is in the tones themselves. It does not strengthen or ennoble this perfect glory of an action which takes place in the skies to fetter it to what Bell calls "the lovely plains of earth" by supposing that its chief meaning is in terms of human joys and woes. And besides, it isn't true. Burney said long ago that when we think we are yearning for the unutterable we are really yearning for the next note.

There are two values, as I see it, in this sort of affective response, which I think is indubitably the one that is appropriate to music and the one that we really feel, even when we think we are responding to some other appeal. The first is that it is idealistic, unselfish; the values are in a realm of idealistic thought that is remote from the clamor of self-interest. The second value, already stated, is that out of such affective experience comes a sensitive, heightened, but wholesomely balanced emotional state, far different from the turbulent and unbalanced emotions that spring from the realm of human affairs.

This response is aesthetic instead of realistic: we enjoy beauty rather than become interested in drama. There are two factors of beauty in music—and two only that I can find. One is beauty of tone, the other is beauty of tonal design; by the latter word I mean all that the tones do. Of course those arouse in us an emotion of beauty—but I am speaking now of beauty as in the object, not the response to it within us. These two factors correspond to color and form, or design, in painting. Artists do not accept the story interest —or as they call it, the illustrative interest—as intrinsic in the purpose of their art, anymore than I accept it as intrinsic in the purpose of ours.

My subject licenses me only to inquire into the nature of music—an aesthetic question—and into its function in human life—a social or humanistic question. But I am irresistibly tempted to say a few words, in the light of the foregoing discussion, on how to "put it over"—a pedagogical question.

Children are capable of a loving regard for beauty. We do not appear to believe this, for we treat children mainly as though they had only appetites and low-grade interests: but a child can move into a realm of beauty and wonder stirred by a rainbow, a rosegarden or the tones of music, quite as quickly as can an adult. I think we music teachers should be a regenerate sort of Pied Pipers and lead them there. If aesthetic feeling is as wholesome and redeeming an influence as I think it is, nothing else that we might do for them is half so important.

Being in a sensory stage, the child can first appreciate beauty of tone. Let us lead him at once to produce it, value it, require it. Let us have him "bathe his ears in tone," as T. P. Giddings has felicitously expressed it. That is genuine musical training. No true artist ever ignores the necessity for that first essential factor of musical beauty. Further, the pure, beautiful tone is the only one that is true in intonation, so it is a prerequisite to fine tonal discrimination, or ear-training. Moreover, it is good for him vocally; and it is a solid foundation for musical appreciation—indeed, it is a degree of appreciation of music, which is, I believe, what formal music appreciation seeks to develop. Above all, let us not throw these values away by becoming teachers of texts, of drama, of elocution, of declamation, because of holding false aesthetic doctrines that have grown in our minds unnoticed. Appreciation of music that is *all music*—of Bach fugues, of Beethoven quartets, of Brahms symphonies—can never grow out of the early misconceptions of the nature and purpose of music which a strongly dramatic approach gives. In fact, it seriously interferes with, if it does not prevent, the growth of such true understanding. The songs do have texts, but so do they have those elements that alone make all music, instrumental as well as vocal, namely, tone and tonal design. They and the text are not incompatible or mutually exclusive, but we should emphasize the tonal elements, because, after all, we are *music* teachers and *music* and its message are our chief concern.

Other subordinate aims or immediate objectives sometimes divert us from the central and highest aim possible, namely, the development of a passionate and understanding love of musical beauty. These I can mention but not discuss. Like the one analyzed, they all have value, are not incompatible with the central aim, and probably attain greater potency when included in the common denominator of a search for beauty than when separately cultivated. They are sight-singing, development through rhythm, vocational training, the recreational use of music. These and others are discussed in the report previously referred to, contained in the Fourth Yearbook of the Department of Superintendence.*

Music will not achieve its highest function in life until it overcomes some dangers from without that are probably greater than those that are within our circle. Without becoming pessimistic—for our subject, after all, gains wider acceptance year after year—we must yet recognize that the orientation of thought and feeling that are largely prevalent in the world today, and that characterize the major part of its action, are somewhat alien to our type of thought and feeling. I mentioned this at the beginning of my paper. The condition would not be ominous, however, were it not for the fact, which also was mentioned, that educational thought has moulded itself into respectful accord with this outside philosophy—or rather this conventional habit of thought. Because educational thought has so moulded itself, however, we find ourselves unsupplied with an adequate or even relevant psychology of feeling, and are con-

---

* See footnote, page 52.

stantly being disquieted by certain educational pronouncements of considerable authority. At best these express regard for our subject but palpably do not understand it; at normal they ignore it completely but disclose a conception of life and education that entirely excludes and discredits our subject and all art; and at worst they gravely discuss the worth of music and prescribe a course of study in it, but in terms that either lack understanding or are little short of being loftily patronizing.

The attempted application of a non-applicable psychology and pedagogy to our subject has led to several inadequate theories or appraisals of it, two only of which I shall mention. In one it is appraised in connection with the theory of social needs or social utilities. The shortcoming in this doctrine, as it appears to me, is that it seems unable to raise its eyes to anything higher than man and his respectable daily routine. I find no suggestion in it that man need live in relation to anything higher than the top of his head, or move in obedience to any impulse higher than to acquit himself in life with credit in the eyes of his fellows, and with financial compensation adequate to the continued maintenance of his respectable station. Again I find nothing progressive in it. It assumes, if I understand it, that life as at present organized in the United States is a complete and final settlement of the problems of human living, and that all that is necessary or desirable is to minister to its needs—to supply, so to speak, the staples which its market demands.

Against this, I believe, is the fact that progress can come only as it has always come, from devotion to ideals that lie far beyond and above the circle of established custom. The movements that have lifted life to higher significance, greater aspiration, have come from men who had visions of principles far above utilities, whose eyes rested not upon this earth, but upon a new heaven and a new earth that, could men but rise above themselves, would be theirs to occupy. Moreover, the doctrine disquiets and chills me, as I puzzle over it—though I may be wrong—by picturing life in terms of what Willem van de Wall calls disintegrated personality. It is true that modern life is excessively complex, many-faced, and that we sometimes feel that we almost lose our personality, our identity, in the many diverse parts that we are daily constrained to play. Swift pace and constant change tend to make life histrionic: we change characters until, like Peer Gynt, we cannot find a solid, permanent core which is ourselves. It is precisely to combat this that we need art and religion: not art with which to attend the Friday night symphony concerts, or religion with which to go to church on Sunday, but art and religion as principles of truth and beauty. As such they can serve as leading motives, around which we may group in symmetry the otherwise jarring notes of our lives. Such integration of personality, music is peculiarly able to effect. Nevertheless, I do not find it mentioned in discussions of music as a social utility; but it seems to me both a greater function and one more nearly in keeping with the nature and purpose of art.

The other doctrine about which I would say a word is that of music as a factor in the worthy use of leisure. Quite apart, from any relation to music, this doctrine appears to me, as it is usually presented, to imply a serious indictment of our scheme of civilization. The implication is that man's work and the real interests of his heart have become separated. If this is true, work, then, has no longer life-giving elements of joy in it: and man must seek to make himself whole by what he does outside of his working hours and working interests.

♦

What is music? It is essentially beautiful tones, related to one another in forms of significance and beauty. All art can be thus reduced to relating things outside ourselves to one another, that we may take pure and unselfish joy in beholding their beauties of relationship; just as all utilitarianism can be reduced to relating the things outside ourselves to ourselves, that we may take advantage, material good, or profit from the relationship. To relate mass to mass, color to color, line to line, and, in music, tone to tone—this is the passion of artists; Maupassant puts it in a short clause: "that search for seductive forms which is art."

What is the function of music? I will state it in the language of that Fourth Yearbook, cited earlier: "To contribute to the character of the individual and society an additional measure of the idealism, the joyous preoccupation with unselfish interests, the elevation and purification of feeling, and the psychic health dependent upon abundant but orderly expression of emotion, that come from appreciative contact with, and endeavor to create or recreate, the beautiful in Music."

THE VALUES OF MUSIC

> *From Mr. Earhart's "Response for the Conference" to the address of welcome at the thirteenth meeting of the Music Supervisors National Conference, held in Philadelphia, Pennsylvania, March 22–26, 1920.*

WE ARE GATHERED TOGETHER IN THE NAME OF MUSIC. What charm has that name that it can so move us all to this present accomplishment? What values do we all discern? What vision holds our faith?

If you will bear with me for a moment or two, I should like to essay an answer to these questions. If in this answer I seem for a moment to doubt the righteousness of some of our claims for music, it is not because I hold in light esteem the values of music, but because, on the contrary, I prize them so highly that I would protect them against misrepresentation or counterfeit. Base metal must not be circulated for gold, lest gold lose its standard of worth. Values must not be claimed for any and all phases of musical practice lest the priceless values that do inhere in certain of its phases become discredited.

We are likely to speak as though we believed that if music were present in sufficient quantity the vexing problems of human life would all be solved, and a redeemed world would move forward, singing, to its salvation. I, too, have joined in this paean of praise; and, allowing for all the exaggeration characteristic of our enthusiastic race, I acknowledge belief now in a sound basis of truth under the vision. But the unenthusiastic lay public does not so readily concede our claims; and certain embarrassing facts often confront us that must be explained before our own faith can be untroubled and secure. Where music has been present in richest measure we do not always find the most complete redemption. The nation that has been most devoted to music is Germany, but the whole world has seen how she has lost her own soul instead of finding it. The individual musician, as we find him, may be no better than his fellows; often, indeed, the layman suspects that some taint of Bohemian laxity prevails among artists that makes them worse; and musicians, and even school music supervisors, may at times hardly dare to point to themselves in illustration when they would assert the beneficent influences exerted by music upon humanity. I modestly confess this, for one.

Yet will our ancient faith, that Goodness, Truth, and Beauty are somehow allied, not down; and yet, I believe, is that faith justified. The fault is not in the true nature and possibilities of art, but in the false interpretations that man places upon it, and the human shortcomings that hamper him in following its high call. I believe that if we could clarify our vision and clearly distinguish between the natural trend of art and some natural tendencies of the human soul that are prone to become associated with it, we would be prepared to gather new vision, new sense of direction, and increased power for good.

Art, then consists of two elements: one the earthly thought, interest, circumstance, emotion, that clings in the mind at the moment, and that may be taken as the avowed subject of the composition; the other a form of expression, quite detached from the earthly circumstance, that seeks to attain grace, beauty, divine fitness and proportion of a quite idealistic kind. How much of the labor of man has been spent in obedience to this impulse to work, like the omnipotent Creator himself, toward the creation of ideal beauty. How patiently, how cunningly, how unceasingly He has wrought to pose line with line—mass with mass, color with color, tone with tone, word with word—in order that shapes, forms, designs would result that meet this haunting demand of our souls for ideal beauty! The impulse is present in every-day life today, but how little we notice it. Yet in the placing of the furniture in every room, the fashioning of every garment, the planting of every flower garden, we are selecting, rejecting, choosing, in obedience to this craving for fitness, for the rightness in the relations of things to one another, quite beyond their relation directly to our utilitarian needs.

Both of these elements—that which would speak of our worldly experiences, and that which would strive for the creation of ideal beauty—are likely to be present in almost any musical composition. But how greatly do the proportions vary!

Beauty of tone to enchant the ear, symmetry and grace of tonal line to delight the mind, purity and nobility of mood to exalt the spirit, may all be well-nigh absent from the song of a cheap, vaudeville "artist." He may be merely relating, in vulgar tone and vulgar language, some commonplace experience in human life; and how greatly we err if we imagine that the interest of almost any circumstance he could use will atone for the absence of sheer beauty. On the other hand, an organ fugue of Bach's or a string quartet of Beethoven's may lift its feet from earth and wing its way serenely and gloriously in an ecstasy of contemplation of pure beauty. And in a tone-poem of Debussy we may find an almost even balancing of proportions.

There is no intention to suggest that we should choose between two styles of composition, and become either devotees of Bach alone or worshippers at the shrine of the musical futurists. Both elements exist in some proportioning in the greater part of all music, and they are not incompatible. The question is, which is the essential and characteristic element in musical composition, and which holds the greater promise of exaltation for the spirit of man. Upon that element we should fix our attention, and to bring about greater appreciation of it should be our endeavor.

Now I believe that a large part of the failure of music is due to the fact that its emotional and worldly aspects have been stressed much too greatly in comparison with its idealistic aspects. To intensify the emotions of human life may tend to energize life, but not to uplift and purify it. On the other hand, to enlist the spirit of man in a quest for a beauty that is above the earth, that is purely ideal, is to create moods of aspiration and lofty striving that tend to ennoble and dignify human life.

We who deal with your children in the public schools are faced by some difficulties and by some advantages that are peculiar to the situation. We deal always with the song—and the words of the song are likely to fetter it to earth. Because of these words we are likely to come to the conclusion that we are teaching love of nature, the domestic and social virtues, patriotism, and so forth; and I earnestly hope we are teaching all of these; but I hope we are teaching something more. Our work is carried on by grade school teachers who know more about the normal reactions of human beings to the circumstances of life than they know about tonal processes, and who therefore are likely to accentuate the literary and emotional aspects of songs more than they accentuate the purely musical facts—sometimes even to the point of ignoring musical demands entirely. On the other hand we are dealing with children who have no uneasy background of dramatic emotional experience in life. They love tone and rhythm and melody as they love the sunshine, a flower or the rainbow—because it is lovely. They sing, as the boy-choir soprano sings, for pure joy in the beauty of it, and not as the dramatic soprano sings a sacred ballad in church —to bring her sentimental, earth-laden cares to the attention of Omnipotence. Their ears are keen and unspoiled, their receptivity to all we have to bring them almost infinite. If we build on the foundation they bring to us, and do not endeavor to lead them into a conception of art that is based upon our greater worldly experience, they are in a fair way to reap a rich and beautiful harvest from their musical instruction.

And after we have come to love the true aesthetic element, rather than revel in worldly experience, there is another love we must learn. That is love for the best that is in the souls of men and in the souls of little children. If we can discern the beautiful soul of Music, through all her disguises, and discern the beautiful thing that is the soul of Childhood, under all its complex appearances, and if we can then unite the two, we will have performed what we believe is a worthy task, and one that is full of promise for man and for music as a valuable element in the life of man.

MUSICIANSHIP AND MENTAL DEVELOPMENT

The full title of this paper was "Musicianship and Mental Development Through General Music, Vocal." Mr. Earhart would not object to the abridgement used here. In fact, he coveted any device that would "clear the decks for both writer and reader. . . . In this paper, I trust I have made clear that I am indifferent as to whether pupils are taught, or as to whether they learn by laborious, independent thinking or by a goodly measure of imitative processes. . . .

"The strength of teaching, as of learning, is not defined in terms of the laboriousness or independence of the path of approach, but is defined in terms of the mental content gained. If that is vivid, accurate, permanent, the teacher has taught and the learner has learned. . . . Mental action has not been lost, whatever the process of acquisition, because, in any case, the mental action that is strongest and most significant is the ultimate one, the one that cannot and does not begin until after the content is learned." The paper was presented at a general session of the 1931 meeting of the Eastern Music Supervisors Conference (now MENC Eastern Division), Syracuse, N. Y., and is reprinted from the 1931 Yearbook.

WHEN CHOOSING THE TITLE for this paper, "Musicianship and Mental Development Through General Music, Vocal," it did not occur to me that the mental nature of music in general needed support. In fact I must plead guilty to having cherished a belief that music was more purely mental than most of the things with which we concern ourselves. One reason, as I thought, was that which is expressed in the accurately worded statement of Langhans when he says that music, in view of "the incorporeity of its material, the quickly passing tone, and in the absence of a prototype and corrective in the visible world surrounding us, is justly called the most subjective of the arts." So conceiving it, I was, and still am, unable to understand where it exists if it does not exist in the mind. Does it have only an occasional and transient existence? Does it live only while the hall is lighted and the instruments are sounding—and is it dead when the lights are out and the musicians have gone home? If it is not dead, where does it live? Where, for instance, does Beethoven's Fifth Symphony live, outside of the brief moments when some orchestra somewhere happens to be playing it? I had fancied it lived between times in mind, the very domain that gave it birth without the least bit of aid from anything in the external world. I had even thought that I found it at times present in my own mind, day and night, long after the books were closed and the lights out.

But you all believe this, even as I. The question is, rather, whether you appraise this sort of mental content in the same terms and as highly as I do. Is the capacity of the mind thus to hold and deal with musical imagery a mental weakness or a mental power? If it is a power, is it the one that President Eliot had in mind when he said that music was the best mind-trainer in the list? Or is there some other power, fancied or real, which has underlain the claims advanced by him and by others in behalf of music as strong mental nutriment? An article by Dr. Jacob Kwalwasser* in the *Music Supervisors Journal* raised these questions afresh and has made it difficult for me to get on with the specific business of my paper until they are answered in some fashion. In trying to answer I am not taking issue with Dr. Kwalwasser. On the contrary I am as much disposed as he to attack the claims of music as a mind-trainer, so long as the basis of the claims is that which he singles out for attack. But I believe there are other claims upon which the mental strength of music may be fully justified, and it is to the exposition of these claims that we now turn. Since they have received little or no attention up to the present, however, it will be necessary first to examine our system of thought, in order to ascertain why they have been so neglected.

The root of the difficulty, I believe, lies in an obsession on the part of the modern world with one type or direction of mental action which is so great that it excludes from our vision any and all other types or directions of mental action. That dominating type or direction of mental action is the one which we commonly call scientific. It is also termed rational, or rationalistic, but as those

---

* Jacob Kwalwasser: "Do You Believe in Fairy Stories?" *Music Supervisors Journal* (now *Music Educators Journal*), Vol. XVII, No. 3 (February, 1931), p. 21.

terms hold connotations some of which are erroneous, they are less suitable to our purpose and we shall accordingly use chiefly the term scientific.

Now the scientific is characteristically concerned with facts about the material universe. Bergson says that the rational intellect was formed on matter and its purpose is the manipulation of matter. If you call up a vision of the scientist in your imagination you see him with implements and instruments and in the presense of matter which he is observing. I am not belittling the strength, even the majesty, of the scientist's methods. What I would have you observe is that at present you see him dealing with externals; that you recognize his first purpose to be that of getting at material facts; and that you concede to sensation, perception, observation, (accurate, by implication) high place in his methods. The old education, as Jacob Kwalwasser truly says, attached great value to mind-training. I would point out now that the newer education has come to define mind-training as resident in the scientific method just described, and as resident in that only, and has, more unfortunately, befogged us all because it has not even completed the true picture of mental action under scientific method.

For observe that at the point at which we stopped we had not yet come upon *thought*. It is understood to be there, it is understood that all of these earlier processes are but to pave the way for it and that they would be empty, barren, did it not follow, yet education has been singularly reticent about discussing it. The explanation probably is that education, in this country, has been largely based upon animal psychology. A very eminent educator gave me that as his opinion, as we talked in Detroit. Surprisingly, in a moment of casual reading one evening last week, after this paper had been half written, I came upon additional statements of the kind in an excellent article in the *Phi Delta Kappan*, written by Coleman R. Griffith. I dare not stop to quote, but the conclusions, which are inescapable to anyone who accepts the premise, may be stated. Animal psychology has focused our attention upon learning, and even upon mechanical learning, as by conditioned reflexes. Knowledges and skills it can and has dealt with. On reflection, ideation and thought, through which the knowledge gained functions in discovery, in creation, and in building individuality as against mass production of a standardized humanity, it has perforce remained silent, because animals are not original thinkers. As a result all that is most distinctively and profoundly and nobly human has received too little attention in the educational world, and many of us are suffering from what we feel is an incongruous and unpleasant mechanicalism and spiritual shallowness in school work.

Acquisition of knowledge, then, is not the strongest or highest use of mind, and development of learning power is not the highest form of mind-training. We reiterate, too, that these proceed by present reactions to present stimuli, and that the stimuli are characteristically external. The mind-training by means of music which Kwalwasser rightly scorns is probably thus conceived as knowledge about, and skill with, staff-notation or instruments; or factual knowledge of composers, chords, forms, history, or whatnot, as presented in textbooks. So far as training the mind is concerned these facts are no better or no worse than similar knowledge would be of butterflies or grasshoppers, or the forms, weights and sizes of all tin cans in the world; and, indeed, since such knowledge is valuable *not* for its reaction on mind but for utilitarian purposes, the knowledge of tin cans might be the better.

But just as learning implies dealing with externals, with the objective world, so does reflection, ideation, imagination, thought, imply dealing with that which lies in the inner or subjective world, where it represents the accumulated result of all the learning and all the experience that has preceded. Here we come upon the individual and the unique; for no two minds are stocked quite alike (however we teachers try to stock them), and mental metabolism is such that were the mental stocks identical the products made of them by individual reflection would be different. Consequently, in reflection, ideation, thought, lies all that wealth of individual creative power which Hughes Mearns is revealing; and it is that which has given the world all the improvements, spiritual as well material, which it has ever received from man. Moreover, this final mental action is the strongest that is possible to the mind, because it requires a concentration, a control, a range and a purposive quality that the world of sense does not furnish.

The stuff of learning, then, is the outside world; the stuff of thought is the world of ideas within. Some ugly images, some unclean spirits, some distorted forms, will come to haunt our chambers of ideas, because such things are present in the outward world and we may not be wise enough to exclude them; but that is another story. Just now I would emphasize the fact that the sign of thought is withdrawal from the world of sense, and the sign of observation and factual learning is an acute awareness of that world. The more intensely we reflect and think, the more we withdraw and concern ourselves with a content that emerges from a silent treasure-house within.

If thought is concerned with an inner content, the question remains whether the specific nature of that inner content is an index to the strength of thought, or, whether the energy of functioning is the index. In character the function appears to be a kaleidoscopic (though purposive) turning over of images and ideas deposited to date by experience, until they fall into some significant, arresting conclusion, pattern or creation. With an Edison the mental content may be chemicals, metals, reactions of substances of various kinds under various kinds of forces. They turn in his mind, under the spell of that roving, exploring type of thought or meditation that someone has designated as the unfailing sign of creative action, until they form new connections or assemblages, and, behold, a new invention is born. With a Beethoven the mental content is tones, rhythms, melodies, harmonies, tone colors, forms. They race unceasingly through his mind, compel his attention to themselves as insistent inner voices, until at length they compose themselves into a form that is irresistible in its glowing compulsion and literally *must* be set down. With a painter the mental content is hues, colors, lights, shades, masses, forms. In all these, however, the mental function is the same; and the question is whether the mental power that is evident is not rightly expressed in terms of the function rather than in terms of the content used. It seems to me that it is. A Beethoven is not less nor is he more, as a mental engine, than an Edison, a Michelangelo, or a Bismarck; although the materials of his thought lie, of course, in a widely different field. Here, it may be, we find the source of that generic resemblance that may be observed among all great men, no matter how different their fields of endeavor. They are all distinguished alike by their capacity for abstract thought, for their ability to concentrate upon and fashion thought out of the world of images which they carry within themselves. They absorb the world and are not absorbed in it. Contrary to popular thought, they are fully alive to this present world; but it is a world that does not engross them as an overwhelming spectacle, but instead is conquered and immured in the mind. There it is pondered and assimilated, or, by a subtle alchemy, it undergoes mysterious transformations in meaning. In the highest outcome it issues as a world reinterpreted and reborn. But—and I can not say it too strongly—the sign of this greatest and most precious kind of mental action is that it functions upon a content of ideas. True, those ideas were once observations, facts, experiences, but as such they commanded the individual. They can not be commanded by him until he has captured and chained them within himself, there to refine and reshape them and marshal them into cohorts that wear the uniform of his individuality.

Meumann, in his book, *The Psychology of Learning*, occupies himself chiefly with a discussion of imprinting. Obviously what is not imprinted is not learned; and the strength of learning may here be defined in terms of the vividness, accuracy and permanency of the imprinting. We have seen that this is not the end of mental action; but the first condition of future ideation is that vivid, accurate and permanent imprintings shall have been made.

Here, as I see it, we can enter upon the study of music as a factor in mental development; for nothing, unless it is the scintillant lines traced by a fireworks display, or the evolutions of an airplane squadron, or other such movements through space, can equal in fascination and deep impress upon memory the movements of tones through time. That appeal to memory and ideation, backed, as it is, by powerful emotional reactions, is a value which I think we have overlooked, or at least have underestimated. Our oversight is probably due to the prevalence of those same eastwinds of animal psychology and scientific outlook which we deplored earlier. Through them we have been led to the study of musical sensory powers, to the teaching of factual knowledge about music, skill in sight singing, skill in playing instruments, information about composers, and such matters, and to consider these as synonymous with the mental content of music, all unmindful of the mental power and control that inheres in attending sensitively to, and remembering vividly, accurately and permanently, all that makes entrance to the mind through the avenue of hearing. To possess a stock of aural imagery or tonal memories, and to have acquired a tendency toward musical imagination, that is to say, a desire to commune with these wraiths of music that people the chambers of the mind, is to have laid the foundations of true musicianship and, better still, to have started the mind on those habits of control, reflection, thought, that are the essential possessions of the educated individual.

How much of such fundamental organization of the minds of children around a core of music can be done in connection with General Music Vocal? In principle, all of it; in degree, as much as conditions and the powers of the teacher permit. By what processes? That question is not so readily answered in the limits of one paper, but you have a right to expect me to reply.

The essential condition of ideation is absence of objective stir. The mind cannot recall sensitive images while the senses are being assaulted by fresh excitations. The atmosphere of the school musicroom must therefore be one conducive to the flow of musical ideas. Distracting sights and sounds must be avoided, just as they are at a concert before the music begins. Even music itself must be so produced that it seems to address the mind behind the ear rather than the ear itself; for do not doubt that it may be produced in so hard-shelled and external a way that it effects no entrance into the world of ideas. In such case it discloses its hard externality by ugliness, roughness, and deviations from pitch and rhythm that persist in spite of any number of repetitions. Unmusicalness, in short, is always a sign that the producers are in a stage of musical *sensation,* not musical *ideation.*

A thousand tricks are at the hand of the wise and musical teacher to help her in reaching the source of the child's musical imagery. She will not rely upon injunction and command, for to do so will compel attention to the teacher, but will rely upon the engaging power of music itself. Her own mind will be attuned to what is coming next, and will be singing. Her mind, I say, and not her voice; although her voice may participate, in accompaniment, if it will do so discreetly and not overpower the singing in the mind—as actual voices of singers have a habit of doing. When she is sure that the ideational minds of the children are engaged and are ready to prompt the singing, *and not until then,* she will let them begin. She will know this moment just as any good conductor of an a cappella chorus or the leader of a string quartet knows of a certainty when all the minds of his group are already filled with the clear image of that first tone; he seems almost to hear its presence behind those silent faces with their fixed and introspective eyes.

Can children so lose animal concern with heterogeneous surroundings and live in a world of quick and complete ideation? Yes; they followed the Pied Piper, you remember, and knew not what was to right or left of them. And lest you think I am describing some sort of a loose-fibred dream-state or trance-state, in which the intelligence is asleep, I will define it further. The intelligence is not asleep, it is rather concentrated. To all that has to do with the moving tonal lines upon which the attention is passionately fixed, the intelligence and the rational intellect are keenly responsive; but they are dead to all else. The faculties are, emphatically, not dulled, they are rather integrated with feeling and vision, and the child is whole. Precisely such complete integration and co-ordination of all powers, physical, mental and spiritual, on a high plane of activity, is experienced by every artist when concentrated upon his art-task; and it was the one President Eliot had in mind when he said that the best example of the coordination of all those powers, which he specified as I have done, was to be found in a man playing the organ. The organ; for neither the intellect nor the body may abandon the spirit there.

To evoke these memories of tone, these wraiths of tone that move in remote and quiet recesses of the mind, requires a degree of concentration, of fixation of attention, that is most uncommon in the schoolroom. At times when I have asked children to remember a curious phrase, played once, quietly, in a way that invited them to store it in their stock of memories rather than to hear it with their ears, I have felt that I could almost sense the workings of their minds. This concentration of attention differs, too, from almost any other that is gained in the schoolroom, because it is involuntarily, happily given. The pupils are charmed, not startled or coerced, into attention. The signs of the state, which may be easily secured by any teacher at almost any time, are a stillness of body that resembles that of a deer whose ear has caught a distant sound. Even the eyes stop moving, grow fixed, and acquire depth instead of that hard opaqueness that characterizes the glance of the youngster whose eye is running over the surface of things. The discipline, of course, is perfect. The effort to invoke one impalpable tone to come forth quiets a class more than would hours of commands or a threat to keep them after school. It might be well to add that it even quiets them more effectively and more enjoyably than would a phonograph record played, or a concert overture performed on piano. And it may not be amiss to say that I think such intense invocation of tonal memories as I have described is mind-training.

Our animal psychology has so impressed us with the alleged fact that children are little animals and primitives that we have almost lost sight of the fact that they are really little thinkers and artists with remarkable understanding and intelligence. I grant that results, given a poor teacher who begins work on animal-psychology premises, often appear to confirm the doctrines of the grisly school of education. But given a teacher who has understanding, spiritual penetration, and artistic musical fibre, unsuspected depths of those same qualities will be disclosed in the children.

The integration of faculties of which I spoke is so real, and it provides a mental engine of such power, that none need fear that sight singing and a knowledge of such facts as that two sharps form the signature of the keys of D major and B minor must be omitted. *Those* matters can be taught without stirring the ideational, reflective and creative depths of the pupils at all—and usually are so taught—but it is difficult to really stir those depths, not merely sentimentally pretend to do so, and then escape a spirit of inquiry, an eager acquisitive action of the intellect, that will fructify in knowledge and power. The reasons (for there are more than one) are, first, that knowledge so related to vital experience has significance, value. It is to premature technical study what study of irises is compared with noting the color of your sweetheart's eyes. Secondly, the pattern, the illustration of use, being fixed as an unforgettable example in the mind, will recur again and again, and will be subjected to endless analyses which will tend to illuminate and verify many succeeding facts. For instance, you who are here are asked, we will say, to give an account of 5/4 measure. How fortunate it is that you have one piece in your minds (and probably only one!) that you can call forth and study! And Russia is far away, too, and Tchaikowsky's hand has long been still.

In a final paragraph, I will try to sum up my faith.

I am indifferent as to whether pupils are taught, or as to whether they learn, by laborious, independent thinking or by a goodly measure of imitative processes. Rational drive of the mind against an obdurate wall of facts is not the highest type of mental effort anyway, and it is certainly not the type that is appropriate in teaching and learning music. Moreover, the strength of teaching, as of learning, is not defined in terms of the laboriousness or independence of the path of approach, but is defined in terms of the mental content gained. If that is vivid, accurate, permanent, the teacher has taught and the learner has learned. Mental action has not been lost, whatever the process of acquisition, because, in any case, the mental action that is strongest and most significant is the ultimate one, the one that cannot and does not begin until *after* the content is "learned." Once learned, imprinted, the processes of imagination and thought must be put in operation, *not* as automatic recall and only after so many rote repetitions that a blank phonograph record would inescapably catch and yield them, but as a lively, thoughtful, highly conscious return, with interest, of that which the mind had caught. Such ideational and reflective dealing with mental content is of the highest value. Any subject so taught that its content passes from the transient sensational stage to the permanent ideational stage adds distinctly to the mental power of the learner. Music is well fitted for such teaching and learning because the atmosphere of feeling with which it is invested gives it extraordinary power to unlock the gates to receptivity and so gain permanent place in the affections of the mind. Its full value is not realized, however, if it is left to slumber in the place it has gained. It must be recalled, be made to live again, and to take its place with others of its kind and fall into organized, clearly understood, working relations with them. When it and its fellows do this, the possessor is learning music; and to prompt all this chain of action from the beginning is the business of the one who is called upon to teach music. And I do think the process inescapably involves the mind.

THE INTEGRATED EDUCATIONAL PROGRAM

This paper, one of the later writings of Will Earhart, was prepared for the 1934 National Convention of the Music Educators National Conference. This, indeed, was the year that the name of the Conference was changed from Music "Supervisor's" National Conference to Music "Educators" National Conference. Though the fact is not put forth in any of the material printed in this book, it is true that Mr. Earhart was one of the hearty supporters of the change of name and the change of description and philosophy represented by the adoption of the new name.

Never what one might call humorous in his steadfast adherence to his philosophy and beliefs, Will Earhart nevertheless had disciples—of whom there are many hundreds—who will point out the lightness of touch which made Will Earhart's sometimes isolated position tenable to himself as well as to his listeners and readers.

There are other writings in this book which deal in a general or specific way with related or similar subjects. The purpose of these brief sketches interpolated in the book is to introduce and not to explain. Thoughtful readers who have probed the depth of Mr. Earhart's thinking as represented in these articles need no further introduction than the opportunity to read, study and evaluate.

IT MAY BE WELL for us to agree in advance as to what this paper is about. As I think of it, indeed, we may be able to agree better on what it is about before I begin than after I have finished. My speeches, I find, often have that peculiarity. But in this case it is more than ordinarily important, because even I do not know. And while I have become accustomed to uncertainty on the part of those who listen, I do like to feel clear about it myself—for a long enough time, at least, to enable me to get started.

When the Research Council was meeting in Cleveland some six weeks ago, it developed that this section program lacked one speech to make it standard size. I was asked to act as interstitial material. The topic suggested was, as I understood it, Integrating the Music Program in the Elementary School. Having heterodox views on that subject—or, at least, views that are heterodox according to Spring Styles in Pedagogy for 1934—I demurred. I proposed instead, Contributing and Enriching Factors in the Elementary School Music Program. I do not believe the committee liked that subject, but I was the only bidder and they were helpless; so that, for the weekend, became the topic. But when I arrived in Chicago and received a copy of the official program, I learned that my subject was—The Integrated Educational Program. That is somewhat worse than the others. Nor does there appear to be time for three speeches on my part, however eagerly you await them, so I have decided to amble around in the generous territory chance has provided me and see if perchance during the speech I may say something on one or more of the topics. I do not guarantee to say anything, you understand. It should always be agreed that no speaker on a pedagogical subject is under obligation to say anything. But that is no reason why a person should not speak.

I

So first let us take a glance at integration. This is sometimes called fusion, and anon, correlation. It recognizes that the Creator lets us look on an entire universe at once, and respond to it completely. It believes, with this in mind, that education is unduly compartmentalized by reason of having subject divisions, and that it does not, therefore, reflect the living, glowing, reality of the world. Life, it would say, is organic and not mechanical. The factors interplay and interpenetrate, and you cannot know any one factor rightly by studying it separately. Therefore, when education dissects the organic whole and presents it, to the child's experience, in rigid subject compartments, it is guilty of an act of abstraction and becomes decidedly artificial.

Now I am in sympathy with this general view of the organic unity of life and education. My heart and my lungs, for instance, are not supposed to be my organs of thought, but if you stop them, or either one of them, my thought ceases as surely as if you had injured my brain. Similarly, geography is not supposed to be the seat of economics, history or art; but take geography away and these have no abiding place and become abstractions. Any geographical item is thus much more than a geographical item. It is alive, and all that is to be found in physical or in human life, as the case may be, is suggested or connoted when we think of it. I must make a willful and painful effort if I exclude from my thought of Mexico, for instance, all except its present geographic form and nature.

The project method, the play-way, and the plans of the progressivists in education, all alike seek to avoid this unnatural and arid compartmentalization. John Dewey, in his Inglis lecture at Harvard some three years ago, wrote eloquently and convincingly against instruction organized in a vertical gradation plan based on separate subjects, as contrasted with that horizontal expansiveness and freedom that should mark a vitalized education. Now the fusionists would secure this horizontal naturalness by mixing contents of subjects. Speaking as musicians, we may say that the one, or subject method, would take a single subject and develop it into a fugue, the other would construct a free fantasia on a number of themes drawn from various sources. But the point I wish to consider is whether this fusionist plan is quite the same as the plans pursued under the project method or by the progressivists; and, if it differs, in what the difference consists. I venture greatly in undertaking such an inquiry and my conclusions are subject to revision as I study more examples of integration than I have yet been privileged to see. Nevertheless, we may at least pose the problem more clearly before our thought by this early inquiry.

As I see it, the project method is superior to integrated study because it characteristically begins with a life situation, broadly conceived, which, being pursued, continually throws the pupils back upon scholastic resources. This is the method of life itself. It has excellent motivation, as life situations always have; and when the pupils are thrown back upon the classroom, there to seek additional knowledge and understanding, each component classroom subject, though it may still be steadfastly pursuing its own individual path of progress, becomes illuminated, meaningful, and integrated with the others. But contrawise, the integrated program appears, at least in some samples of it I have seen, to start rather with the classroom subject matter, and merely to articulate small bits of different subject matters. If this is what integration means, it seems quite as artificial to me as our old friend, correlation—from which, indeed, I am unable to distinguish it. Such short excursions from one realm of interest to another may make for a community of interest among the teachers of a school, and may add some strength to all subjects in the thought of the pupils, because all their teachers then appear to them equally interested in all subjects. That is to say, a social and scholastic integration may take place under these circumstances; and that result in itself has its uses and high values which I cheerfully concede. But integration in a psychological sense, which would seem to me to be of very much greater value, could it be secured, does not yet appear to have taken place.

There is an aspect, also, of such articulated study as I have described, that seems to me yet more unfortunate. A large factor in the education of any person is surely that complete absorption in a subject which, though it be only momentary, puts the learner in touch with the very spirit and essence of the subject. There is a spirit of mathematics, a spirit of music, a spirit of nature study, a spirit of history, which, if we somehow grasp it, illuminates the subject and motivates and directs all our future dealings with it in a way that is of priceless value. Such aesthetic penetration to the soul of a subject cannot be caught from fleeting and casual glimpses of it. One must become, for a time at least, steeped in the subject. Now, no integrationist, I suppose, would urge that all instruction should regularly be fused to the extent that the arithmetic lesson would normally hold as much of music and geography as it would hold of arithmetic and that the music lesson would hold as much of geography and arithmetic as it would hold of music. Everyone must assume, instead, that somewhere at some time a music lesson will be given which is distinguishable, in its degree of emphasis on music, from the other two. But there is a danger, we may suspect, that over-ardent fusionism might fail to give any subject such distinct and characteristic emphasis that its own peculiar atmosphere would be soaked up and become known. This atmosphere, as of the printery, the blacksmith shop, the music studio, the painter's studio, is an educational element in itself. Motivation and large understandings arise out of it, and richness of life issues from the experience of it. Possibly we may be shying at shadows, but unless this core of every subject is taught consistently and fully, a dilettante education may result.

Another aspect of integration deserves our attention. I would emphasize the fact that integration, rightly conceived, must be subjective, not objective. The same child goes to the school, the church, the playground and the movies. In a platoon school, which is the type we have in Pittsburgh, he goes successively to the music room, the art room, the auditorium, the geography class. By some alchemy or mental metabolism these diverse elements become fused because they all center in the same transforming agent. I doubt very much whether they ever accumulate in him in separate layers. That implies a point of view too much like that of the Irishman who stuffed his pigs one day and starved them the next, because he wanted his bacon to have a streak of fat and then a streak of lean. A human mind and personality is not so badly mechanistic as that. So, to scramble subject matter beyond the reasonable bounds that are disclosed from time to time to any versatile-minded, sensitive, and alert teacher, may be, if not wrong, at least superfluous. Was it Talleyrand who said of some act that it was worse than a crime, it was a blunder?

To put the whole case figuratively, and again pursuing gastronomical lines of imagery, we may say that I want to know soup, and the very soul and atmosphere of soup, and I want to know ice cream, and the very soul and knowledge of ice cream. To have this knowledge I must—still figuratively speaking, of course—immerse myself in soup and soak myself in ice cream. If you mix them, objectively, before taking, I do not learn to know soup so well, and I do not learn to know ice cream, but I come to know only ice cream soup. Nor will a spoonful of one alternating with a spoonful of the other give me quite the expert and sharply individualized concepts that I seek. Each must appear distinctively and fully in its own character to educate me properly. They are both part of the meal of life, it is true, and I must integrate them. But that really may be safely left to me. I will do it subjectively.

II

And now let us talk sense for a minute or two. I wish to say that I am emphatically in favor of integration, but I think it may be best attained through projects and progressive education methods, plus a reasonable amount of intelligence, culture, and liberal mindedness on the part of teachers. I think, moreover, that we should begin by integrating various phases of the music program itself. The stiff compartmentalization of vocal as compared with instrumental music, and of music appreciation, creative music, toy orchestra and eurhythmics, is almost tragic. Besides, the school music may be still further shut in by the walls of the schoolroom, at least in the elementary school, and never a breath of the music air freely blowing outside may ever penetrate the crayon-dust-laden atmosphere of the schoolroom. I would not, however, integrate these various features of music by objective mixture, but I would give experience in all of them, in some reasonable proportion, to all children, so that music would appear to be more than interpreting, through the voice, printed symbols from what Henry Turner Bailey called the barbed-wire entanglements of staff notation. Have no fear in case you undertake this complex program, that your work will merely be diffused instead of integrated. Music taught so broadly will not only be integrated in itself, but will connect with the outside world, and will form connections and interpenetrations with other subjects in the school. Moszkowski's Spanish Dance with the toy orchestra; making up text and music on Madame Maeterlinck's The Children's Blue Bird; taking class instruction on the piano, violin, or trumpet; responding to rhythm and moods of music in eurhythmics; hearing a Mozart minuet, from one of his symphonies, played by a great orchestra; do these not suggest a lifting and widening of the horizon such as can never come from pursuing rigidly a course in General Music Vocal?

But where will you find the time? That will be the next question. Take it where you can find it. At first, perhaps all from the General Music Vocal period. As the new features vitalize the child in music, the work will go so much faster that you will have more time for it as the number of minutes decreases. You may later discover, indeed, that your work in General Music Vocal was suffering from that condition of which Alice in Wonderland was apprised. She found a realm, you remember, in which you had to run as fast as you could to stay in the same place.

But before this expansion and integration take place, one other bit of integration must be assured. That is in the mind of the teacher. The limitations of the children are often, perhaps, only reflections of the limitations fixed by the knowledge, or by the belief, of the teacher. If the teacher herself likes to improvise, write and harmonize tunes, if she has played in an orchestra as well as sung in a chorus, if her head and heart are filled with a wide range of the great in musical literature, if she has expressed sensitively in eurhythmics the last lovely detail of rhythm, form and shifting mood, then she will feel their necessity, know their expansive power, and see that the children shall be not less lifted than herself above the dull routine of a restricted subject matter that yields no glimpse of glories that await outside its walls.

III

As a final word, I would point out that integration and correlation find their use characteristically in the realm of the factual. That is to say, departments of knowledge, as viewed in the separate school subjects, present bodies of facts that are segregated, each from the other, in a manner unknown in the world outside the schoolroom. Integration would break down the separation between these bodies of facts and give each larger meaning by associating it with the others. Almost all examples of integration that you analyze will thus be found to seek an association of facts from various fields.

Music, viewed in its essential aspect, is not a body of facts, but is an experience in feeling. That feeling, because of its origin, is not connected with any literal circumstances of daily life, or with any particular time or place, but is connected strongly only with the lovely message that gave it birth. The more sharply we try to connect it with the rational, the concrete, the more certainly we lose it; and losing it, we lose also the value for which music exists in the world. In fact, music, as a state of aesthetic feeling, does not associate with the world of practical knowledge so much as it underlies and colors the whole of experience. It is more comprehensive than circumstance, more vague than fact, and far deeper than knowledge, for it is understanding and vision. Its correlations, then, if it has any, are likely to arise from something extrinsic to its own essential nature, namely, its words, if it is song, or its title or program, if it has no words. This was recognized in the resolutions you adopted yesterday. As music, for instance, we do not know with what the Handel "Largo" correlates. As an aria from his opera *Xerxes*, we can correlate it with ancient Greece, with opera, with London, with musical history, and what not. Since it is "about" a plane tree, we might correlate it with nature study and botany. But while and as we do this, the song is lost from our heads and hearts; and the essence of what it is, namely, music, did not, therefore, participate in the correlation. I wonder whether we would not do better to go to the next class with the music ringing in our heads than with certain pertinent—or impertinent—facts stamped upon our memories because they may possess some relevancy when the recitation in the next classroom begins.

Yet, still, I am an integrationist. I think both values, in some proportion, may be secured. I am convinced, though, that the characteristic value in music, as in any subject, and more in music than in factual subjects, should be cherished and be secured first; and its strength and vitality in its own right are the measure of its value for any and all subsequent integration purposes. For a profound musical experience will overflow the moment, and the boundaries normal to the stimulus, and will have all sorts of future reverberations and repercussions. It will prove prolifically creative. If integration would, therefore, fuse the varied fruits of experience, a good recipe to follow would be: "First get your experience, and when you get it, get a good one."

TO JUSTIFY OR NOT TO JUSTIFY

> *It must be remembered by the reader that in 1933 when this paper was written there were grave doubts about the permanancy of the program of Music Education in the schools. Indeed, in this year only four of the six MENC Division Conferences convened; the Southern and the Southwestern were canceled because of the difficulties of the times when banks were closed, teachers were being paid in script if at all, and there was a general gloom over the land. Will Earhart was one of ten Eastern members who were invited to contribute papers to a symposium, "To Justify Or Not To Justify." Reference is made in this short but effective presentation to another more lengthy paper by Mr. Earhart, "Musicianship and Mental Development Through General Music, Vocal," which appeared in the 1931 Yearbook of the Music Supervisor's National Conference, and is reprinted in this volume, page 62. Other papers and speeches printed herein avouch unbounded faith in the basic values of music in the school educational program—not only for all children but all adults as well—a faith inherent in the steadfast philosophy which was the bulwark of Earhart's life and works.*

CERTAIN ASSUMPTIONS must be made, if we are to clear the ground of our argument from confusion. The first is that music, as we shall speak of it, is assumed to be taught successfully. This is no small assumption, for by "successfully" I mean that music shall be taught in such way that the ends sought by all the arts, namely, enrichment of the personality by means of beautiful moments of experience, shall be attained. The second is that all other subjects of the curriculum shall be conceived as being taught successfully in the manner and degree prescribed for music; that is to say, these other subjects also shall be conceived as making in fact the contributions to human living included within their intentions. In short, we accept the ideals of purposes and attainments held on both sides. Only thus can we conceive the various subjects in their true character, and at the same time rid ourselves of fruitless bickerings over methods of teaching and comparisons of teachers with one another.

With the ground thus cleared, the argument for music, as I see it, may be presented in three sections.

I. Aesthetic

Reality and Aesthetic Responses: If we look at the moon and say that it is round, we think we register a "fact." If we regard it and say that it is beautiful, we think we register something less valid. But since the factual, as the affective, merely records a transaction between a certain type of organism (ourselves), something outside the factual is nothing more than a subjective registration—precisely as is the beautiful. What would the multiple eye of the house fly apprehend as the reality "out there?" What is red light to the ants that Sir John Lubbock saw it slay as though it were some deadly Martian ray? What, now, is matter? What is mathematical reality, under modern physicists and Einstein? We can know of all that is outside ourselves only that which we register, and the nature of that registration is prescribed by what WE are. "Round" and "beautiful" are thus equally valid testimony to something that, so far as we can know it, has occurred in us.

The Depth of the Factual Compared with the Aesthetic: The aesthetic appears to involve us more deeply than does the factual. If only half alive, I can see the factual aspects of matter. The dying man can see that "the casement window slowly grows a glimmering square." Square, indeed, but without depth of meaning. Dr. Richard Cabot points out that in our "devitalized" moments, as when we struggle to consciousness after a disturbed night, a baby is a lump of flesh, a picture is but pigment smeared on canvas. Only when we are most alive, when we respond in greatest depth and volume, is the factual submerged and integrated in the tide of response that we know as aesthetic. Had I time, I should endeavor to prove that the factual (alias the rational) deals characteristically with matter, and for purposes of our material well-being.

II. Intellectual and Educational

So far as the rational enters into the intellectual—and there are many who yet naïvely suppose that the rational is all there is of intellectual action—music engages the intellect only in connection with staff-notation, names, dates, acoustics, and other such factual aridities. But if we turn to all that part of the mind that is not concerned with business, manufacture, science—in brief, with the exact and quantitative—we may find music richly present. I cannot elaborate this view here, but in the 1931 Yearbook is one attempt by me to do so, and in the February 1933 issue of the *Music Clubs Magazine* is another. Suffice it to say here that music is conceived in the mind, is held in memory of the mind, is subjected to reflective, creative, ideational processes in the mind, comes forth as great mental achievements from the mind—for who would say that a Beethoven Ninth Symphony is less great as a mental product than a St. Paul's Cathedral—or a play such as Hamlet (not to mention a Chrysler car!)—and in fact can be found only in occasional and brief and precarious existence in the universe outside of the mind. As stuff for the mind to deal with, it is therefore quite as nutritive as scientific matter—say, as the natural history of the lobster. Not the stuff of thought, but the depth and energy of the function of thought is thus the measure of mental and educational worth.

III. Social

The factual, the rational, the utilitarian, the materialistic, the technological, all have this in common: They aim to do something to our material environment that will enable us to attain a condition wherein we will find ourselves leading the better life. What they are concerned with, therefore, is means toward an end. Factories, automobiles, concrete roads, are not the better life, but somehow we think that we may overtake the better life if we pursue it by means of these.

In contrast, art is a present salvation. The sunset, the song, the upthrown Gothic arch, the painter's dream, are present goods, doing something to bring sensitivity, humaneness, harmony, sweetness, purity, unselfishness, nobility, into our living.

By the first of these vaguely held concepts of life, man has been made a producer—a producer of many things, in ever increasing quantity. He has, indeed, almost come to measure the progress of his society in terms of tonnage.

But Henderson says: "If man is the highest product of creation, then civilization must be judged, not by what man produces, but by the manner of man produced."

Dr. William John Cooper, former United States Commissioner of Education, lately stated in Pittsburgh that technological progress would result soon in a 30-hour work week, filled with mechanical actions that required little training. He said that in view of this prospect the prime concern of education was with those factors that would minister to human betterment and happiness, and as examples of such factors he emphasized only health, education, music and art.

So, our civilization seems destined to move, whether we wish it or not, from one that conceived progress in terms of Man as a Producer to one that conceives Man as the Product; and Education must reflect the world.

As the movement advances, we may expect that music, already amiably accepted because of the persistence in society of certain ineradicable humane instincts, will become fully justified in the consciously accepted creeds of people.

In order to leave no doubt, I would say in closing that I, myself, think a place for music in our public schools is justified.

IS MUSIC IN DANGER OF LOSING ITS IDENTITY THROUGH INTEGRATION?

Will Earhart's ability to go to the core of an issue was recognized by many, including those whose capacity for thinking distinguished them from the "sentimental herd." Always a kindly soul, Will listened and learned, but only mildly contradicted or supported opinions stemming from emotional rather than intellectual viewpoints. Prepared in late 1937 and printed in the 1938 MENC Yearbook, this discussion is still not untimely for the thoughtful reader.

THE CENTRAL PROBLEM, of course, is not whether music may or may not lose its identity in an integrated program, but whether, be that identity lost or retained, the child or youth will profit more from an integrated than from a nonintegrated program. We must be liberal enough to say that music as a delimited subject may well be lost if thereby greater souls are won.

Integration, as conceived by its wisest supporters, seeks nothing less than a thoroughly integrated personality; and by that is meant an individual who moves in life's experiences with intelligence, courage, and easy power, weakened by no failures in assimilation and hampered and distorted by no inner stresses and conflicts. To implement its endeavors in this direction, integration devises one of several types of program, all generically similar, and all differing from the type of curricular program largely current in past years.

It is with the integrated program in particular that this paper is concerned. However, a program is but a means toward an end, and cannot profitably be discussed in what, with respect to the ends involved, is a vacuum. We are, therefore, bound to consider integration as an educational philosophy, to inquire into its attendant psychological implications, and only then to examine its program as an agency toward the ends avowed.

Perhaps this large inquiry can best be furthered in a brief paper by introducing at once two terms employed in a book recently published under the title *Integration, Its Meaning and Application*. This book was written by L. Thomas Hopkins, together with a number of colleagues associated as a Committee on Integration of the Society for Curriculum Study. The terms, as used by Dr. Hopkins, are "subject curriculum" and "experience curriculum." They seem to me extraordinarily apt and useful, and so clearly significant that they need little further definition.

With the subject curriculum we are all familiar. Its chief endeavor, if we interpret it aright, is to provide the student with those materials and abilities, or with those knowledges and techniques, with which he can function later in the world outside the school. The experience curriculum, in contrast, appears to aim chiefly at enlarging, empowering, and enriching the individual himself, at the present moment. To coin another pair of terms, the subject curriculum was focused on *function*, while the experience curriculum is focused on the *functioner*. The comparison could be extended indefinitely, if time permitted. Such terms as "knowledge is power" (which explicitly, by the way, it is not, even if Bacon did say it), "efficiency" (a word once much idolized), and "preparation for life," all connect with the subject curriculum. On the other hand the newer terms, such as "the child-centered school," "creative education," the "unit plan," "mental hygiene," "dynamic personality," and, of course, "integration," all connect with the experience curriculum. Whether, in general, the experience curriculum, so understood, is right or not—and I think that in principle it is unquestionably right—it has come into the world hand-in-hand with the revival of an idealistic philosophy and a psychology at last risen out of its barren prisons of reflexology, because the catastrophes into which our civilization has fallen have made it evident that mankind needs more and other faiths and powers than those upon which it so confidently relied prior to 1914 and 1929. Before that period education fully believed that it was competently supplying every factor necessary for complete and progressive living and could and would carry us into a glorious millennium. Since then, together with philosophy and world thought in general, it has been troubled with growing doubts as to whether it may not have overlooked some essential factors to a complete life.

Returning to the terms "function" and "functioner" and using them to designate the older and the newer concepts, let us search for the values that were overlooked under the function concept, and that perhaps may be found included under the functioner concept. They will not be difficult to discover.

Life conceived as function, then, was usually an impoverished if not a grimly skeletal sort of life, because function was almost always conceived in the mechanistic terms of adjusting one's self satisfactorily to the demands of an existing economic-social order. Function, therefore, had an objective, practical, utilitarian connotation: it was concerned greatly, if not wholly, with the problem of getting on in the world. But life holds much besides such functions. Beyond relations to our fellow man we must inescapably preserve relations with certain abstract and infinite principles. When we love nature, listen to music, aspire to ideals of aesthetic or moral beauty and perfection, we are outside the thought of the function curriculum, if not of the subject curriculum. And yet the thirst for satisfaction of these ideals and desires is the most potent force in life, and in it rests the sole hope for a progressively improving humanity.

The function concept, it should be mentioned, was in full accord with, and was supported by, the materialistic philosophy—variously called realistic, mechanistic, deterministic, atomistic—to which preoccupation with the material world about us, in terms of natural science and technology, had given rise. In Jung's words, thought, which before the Renaissance had been vertical, had become horizontal. Psychology, in turn, took on the hues of this prevailing intellectual climate, became physiological, and concerned itself with stimuli and reactions that could be externally observed and precisely measured; and it thereby still further supported the mechanistic outlook in education. As E. C. Lindeman, in his chapter in the book herein earlier cited,* says: "Contemporary educators have been conditioned in the direction of the mechanics of education. Indeed, they have become so engrossed in tests, measurements, classifications, and other mechanical devices that they have well-nigh lost the ability to think of education in terms of organic experiences leading to organic goals."

Let us ask next where an experience curriculum looks to find

---

* *Integration, Its Meaning and Application.*

organic experiences that lead to organic goals. It is an affront to our intelligences to propound such questions and pretend to answer them in a word or two, but if it must be done, the answer here is suggested by the word "goals." An integrating experience can be obtained only when some goal that has formed in the mind calls forth purposeful activity. Feeling, thought, action then function in terms of complete organic unity (or in what ordinary folks call a wholehearted way), until the goal is attained and the inner demand is stilled. There has been integrated experience, conducive to organic health and power and to a feeling of self-reliance and courage; and in the enterprise knowledge and skill, equal to that which might have been acquired under other methods, have probably been gained. In contrast, a function curriculum, in the aspects of it that we have chosen to describe, is in danger of being either nonintegrative or positively disintegrative, because the goals it sets up are far distant and vague, have no intrinsic interest and give rise to no immediate purpose, and, therefore, may call forth effort that is half-hearted, reluctant, blind, and that frequently is persuaded only by extrinsic motives that grade down at times to the desperately low rank of fear.

The goals essential to integrated response are outwardly of infinite variety, but they are alike in that they must appear rewarding to the students and call forth voluntary effort. Search for these requirements explains the tendency of the integrationist, in common with other progressive educationists, to turn largely to creative projects either initiated by the students or placed within areas of inquiry and effort revealed as highly attractive to them. In a philosophic sense, however, no reward of any kind is possible to any human being, except a reward in feeling. Whatever the extrinsic and phenomenal aspect or form of the reward, it is obvious that it cannot be a reward unless we feel rewarded. This is a fact of greatest significance in education, especially in connection with the theory of integrated experience; yet it has not been emphasized by educational writers, even if it has been voiced. Further, it is of the utmost significance in connection with our discussion of music, because music, like all the arts and everything aesthetic, is cherished precisely because it can and constantly does give highly valued rewards in feeling; and these are clearly recognizable as such and as nothing else, because no tangible or material symbol of reward interposes itself to obscure them. The pursuit and production of music in and of itself can therefore be, to a large percentage of the whole population, one of the most integrating experiences possible to human beings.

But if an integrated experience, conducive to the development of an integrated personality, at least potentially, follows whenever purposeful, dynamic, creative interest directed toward a rewarding goal has been aroused, and if such interest can be aroused within a limited subject area, as, for instance, in music (and we know it can be, for we have seen good teachers inspire **effort and** inaugurate the movement toward an integrated personality through music and through many another subject), then what need is there for an integrated program characterized by correlations of subject matter? Again, a comparatively brief answer only can be hazarded. Integrative action may, it is true, take place within a limited subject area, or indeed, in connection with a microscopically diminutive item of experience. It occurs whenever a man finds his job, whenever a child becomes absorbed in so small a task as moving a chair, whenever we are buried in absorbed movement, mental or physical, toward any goal whatsoever. But integration maintained in relation to one small item or area of experience does not ensure maintenance of an integrated personality in the myriad areas of experience that open more and more widely as we advance through life, or even as the child moves swiftly through the events of one day. To retain unity and integrity in a restricted and homogeneous environment may, therefore, be easy: but to retain them through wide, varied, and ever-changing environments requires strength. Subject compartmentalization accentuates artificially the separateness of areas of human experience: and while an individual is, at least by birth, an organic whole, is a unitary and integrated being, his integrity may well be shattered by such implied contradiction of it and by such powerful tugs upon it. To counteract this tendency the correlated type of integrated program is offered. Nevertheless, for reasons I shall state, I doubt whether it represents a wise solution of the problem. Use of creative projects would at least seem far wiser.

My objection to the correlated program is that, unless very carefully guarded, it secures a unitary type of experience by disintegrating and denaturing the component elements of that experience. The state and habit of mind secured are good, but they are secured too easily. Integration of fragments that are in themselves weak or colorless cannot make for great strength of integrated personality. If subjects taught in restricted subject areas are taught with too great logical severity, with too rigid exclusion of every suggestion that other areas of knowledge exist, and with too great depth of detail—and undoubtedly they often are so taught—that condition can surely be corrected without abducting the subject from its normal environment and approaching it on the basis of its own extrinsic interests and adventitious connections, rather than upon the basis of its own intrinsic interest. Moreover, music, above all the arts, is highly subjective, is "without any prototype or corrective in the visible world surrounding us," as Langhans says—and represents essentially an organization or integration of spirit rather than a body of world facts to be observed. To approach it primarily on the basis of its outward manifestations and connections is similar to making a study of prayer as encountered in various environmental connections and periods and countries without seeking the spirit of prayer. In short, music, in metaphysical terms, is not so much phenomenal as it is noumenal: and to approach it on the basis of its phenomenal aspects is, therefore, an error. This is not to say that it should not function in personal, integrative living and be welded into the "scheme of things entire"; but this can be done through creative projects into which it would fit in its living, noumenal character.

Is music in danger of losing its identity in an integrated program? It may; but integrated programs are of so many varieties that I should have to see the particular program before I could make explicit answer. *Should* music lose its identity in any type of program? That I can answer more definitely, and the answer is an unqualified no. But I welcome the jolt to our thought that integration has given, because music is yet, all too often and in too many places, taught as a system of knowledges and skills, and not sufficiently as a quieting, integrating, frame of thought and feeling in which clashing problems of earth are resolved and the spirit can become whole again.

FUNDAMENTALS IN MUSIC VALUES

This paper was prepared for and read in the meeting of the discussion group on music education at the 1927 Dallas, Texas, convention of the NEA Department of Superintendence (now American Association of School Administrators).

THE SUBJECT ASSIGNED ME is so large, and the time so brief, that I shall be obliged to speak dogmatically. Abundant support could be adduced, however, did the time permit: for the psychology of aesthetic experience, though accorded scant attention in America at this time, is extensive and competent, and the conclusions herein presented might be supported by quotations from many writers, ranging from Schopenhauer, to Bergson and William James, and including Clive Bell, Warner Fite, Vernon Lee, Ethel Puffer, Hugo Munsterberg, Edmund Gurney, and countless others.

Several values of music which might, I suppose, be considered fundamental by some persons, are very generally recognized. One of these is its socializing value. Cooperation upon a plane of elevated feeling and high endeavor and coordination or team work

[NOTE: The final general session at the 1927 Dallas convention of the NEA Department of Superintendence was a concert program provided by the National High School Orchestra, Joseph E. Maddy, organizer and conductor, and a chorus of eight hundred children from twenty-four Dallas elementary school conducted by the Dallas supervisor of music, Sudie L. Williams. This was the second organization of the National High School Orchestra, the first having been for the 1926 convention of the Music Supervisors National Conference at Detroit, referred to elsewhere in this volume. In addition to the concert program for the final general session, the orchestra played at the opening of the fourth session, and short programs were provided for various other sessions by ensembles organized within the orchestra personnel. These included a large string choir, multiple string quartet, brass choir, harp ensemble, and a symphonic band of 100. There was a total enrollment in the orchestra of 267 players from high schools in thirty-nine states. It was at this Dallas 1927 convention at the meeting of the discussion group on music, where Mr. Earhart read the accompanying paper, that the widely quoted resolution was adopted stipulating and enlarging upon four points: (1) We favor the inclusion of music in the curriculum on an equality with other basic subjects. (2) We favor an immediate extension of music study to all rural schools. (3) We believe that an adequate program of high school music instruction should include credit, equivalent to that given other basic subjects. (4) We recommend that this subject (music) shall continue to receive the attention of the NEA Department of Superintendence, and be included in the discussion groups of its annual program.]

that is motivated by singularly self-subordinating ideals of group achievement are certainly represented in extraordinary degree in the performances of choruses, orchestra and bands, such as have been assembled here to contribute to the programs of the Department of Superintendence. No one who can sense the spirit, as they sing and play, of these boys and girls gathered from forty states of our Union, can escape the conviction that all of the social solidarity, mutual understanding, and good will toward which our forefathers valiantly aspired, are budding and blossoming in their endeavor.

The vocational value of music is perhaps not a fundamental one, but deserves passing mention. We should remember that in 1910 the United States census disclosed that only school teachers and physicians and surgeons outranked in point of numbers engaged, those who registered as "Musicians and Teachers of Music." In 1920 technical engineers and trained nurses were, in addition, in numerical ascendancy over musicians and teachers of music: but that condition must be considered as abnormal. If we add to this reliably reported "full-time" vocational use of music the enormous part-time vocational use that is constantly made of it, the vocational strength of the subject must be almost unique.

But we who love and have lived with music, and who teach it to your children, know that these and other recognized values of music are not its essential and characteristic value. Its real value is something quite different and of immeasurably greater significance; and lest this statement should appear to belittle the values already mentioned, I hasten to add that this different and greater value does not exclude those or any others, but embraces them. It is a greater common denominator in which all other values are integrated, nor can the larger value be defined without some comparatively abstruse discussion. In order to define it we must forsake our favorite realm of objective fact and enter the almost forbidden realm of subjective testimony. But please remember that whenever we speak of value at all we must speak in terms of subjective testimony. Facts can be objectively gathered and computed by the rational intellect, but they have no meaning whatever except as appraised in terms of human feeling. Did we have no preferences, facts would have no significance. Value is thus, in its true meaning and very nature, wholly subjective.

Let us approach this part of our inquiry by posing a rather crude antithesis. We live in a vast and complex universe in which sensations, perceptions, experiences, beat in unceasingly upon us. All that touches us may be conceived, and is largely conceived, in terms of its relation to us—to our interests, advantage, purposes. But another outlook is possible. Under its sway, we view all these things of the universe, not in their relation to us, but in their relation to one another, as pure forms, detached, impersonal, significant only in relation to the satisfaction or dissatisfaction they give us as objects of contemplation. Thus the farmer, gazing on the summer sky, in which cloud-masses rimmed with glorious light are drifting, is likely to see not so much what is there as something that may portend to his fields; but his infant son, looking with wonder into that same sky, beholds a vision into which he is drawn in complete absorption. That moment, that vision, is for him complete.

Now these two views are seldom, or never, completely separated, but are constantly mingled, in each one of us and even at the same moment in any one of us, in some proportion or other. Nevertheless they are essentially different and distinguishable. And I need not say that the first (while never untinged by some trace of the second) is the characteristic mode of the industrial scientist, the breadwinner, the utilitarian man that is in all of us, and even of our entire occidental civilization; while the second (though never untinged by some trace of the first) is the characteristic mode of the artist that is in all of us, of the infant, of the child, and to a lessening extent, because the shrewd practicality of a greedy world gradually displaces it, of the youth and the man.

A second illustration, taken from Vernon Lee's weighty little book, *The Beautiful,* amplifies our thought somewhat. It turns on a discussion of the words "good" and "useful" in comparison with "beautiful." "Good" and "useful" are held to be largely synonymous. When we say a road is a *good* road we mean, according to Lee, that it good *for* something, and it furthers some purpose of ours and is therefore useful. Of course any road compared with no road, is useful: but a good road furthers our purpose better and is therefore *more efficiently useful.*

But what is a beautiful road? The main distinction seems to be that a good road is one that *gets us somewhere*—and note that this means *somewhere else,* where we wish to be. A beautiful road, by contrast, may get us nowhere: but on the other hand, if it is beautiful enough, *we do not care to go elsewhere.* We remain, absorbed in contemplation of its beauties.

The beautiful is thus distinguished by the fact that it holds not future advantage but present value. Its worth to the individual has not, it is true, been considered objectively by someone else, as we, say, who are gathered here, might consider it. Nevertheless we may confidently term it a value in this sense: that value is subjective and that the individual experiencing beauty is conceding value to the experience by the mere fact of continuing to prefer it. In short, it must feel like value to him.

But what is its value to us? What are its characteristics? Can we, standing aloof and, examining it critically, attribute to the experience of the beautiful that worth which our constant use in this paper of the word "value" has inescapably suggested? These questions must be answered, even if briefly and dogmatically.

We have seen that the experience of the beautiful is at least not utilitarian. Without time to support our propositions we can, by mere reference to the facts of our own experiences of the beautiful, affirm other characteristic qualities. The effect of the beautiful is unquestionably an emotional, or, it is better to say, an affective one. Our feeling, detached by its peculiar power from utilitarian thought or concerns of life, becomes purified of bitterness, fear, poignant and wayward doubts, annoyances and sorrows. The world of beauty is thus untroubled of earth. But at the same time our feeling, because integrated in and moulded upon the thing which is perfect, instead of upon that which is ugly or disquieting, is exalted, quickened. Its quality differs from emotions aroused by worldly circumstances in that it is high, keen and sensitive, yet poised, balanced and confident. In comparison the emotions of life are poignant, distressing and unbalanced. When we have had experience of the beautiful our ideals have been fulfilled, the world has been proven to hold that which is bright, true and promised of God. In our absorption we have lost ourselves; and oddly, it is at the moment when we have most completely lost ourselves by reason of something that has taken us utterly into it, that we feel ourselves raised to our highest. An excellent analysis of this psychological phenomenon may be found in Puffer's *Psychology of Beauty,* but even were there no scientific explanation, it could be proven as a matter of common experience. Who has not been carried by a symphony, a sky flooded with moonlight, a cathedral, a poem, a drama, a picture, a statue, into a world where the sense of personality grew vague and thin; only to feel a sharp sense of descent, of a shrinkage of his spiritual stature, as he came out of the auditorium into the clanging eager street, and once more took up his personal concerns the while a keen sense of his distinct individuality flowed back upon him.

Do these subjective results have any worth for a world such as we appear to be making today? Or shall we continue to believe that utilitarian thought and labor, if only spurred more feverishly so as to produce more tonnage, will bring about that millennium it so long has falsely promised? Do we not know that self-interest breeds self-interest, that utilitarianism breeds utilitarianism, even as war breeds war? Are we not wise enough to see that striving is not destined to bring about a spiritual goal by preliminary conquest of everything in the world (for there are always worlds left to conquer) but that we must conquer worldliness by becoming less worldly? If we know that youth is not utilitarian but quick to embrace experiences that leave sordid thoughts below them, shall we still deal out these cleansing moments reluctantly and parsimoniously to them?

And now a word about the beautiful in relation to music specifically. This aesthetic value, which is the greatest value, has been largely unrecognized because music, instead of being understood as beauty, has been popularly conceived as emotion. Had words never been associated with music these "emotions of life," as Clive Bell terms them, would have remained, as with architecture or as with the great instrumental works of Bach, Beethoven and Brahms, outside of its circle. I do not mean that ideas and interests of human life, as introduced by song texts, are incompatible with musical beauty. I mean only that they have been mistaken for the essence of music's meaning instead of being recognized as only related factors that derive what glory they acquire almost wholly from the effulgence of a sun that shines in a sky remote from worldly life.

But I need not enlarge upon this topic of the real nature and function of music, for Edna St. Vincent Millay has said more than I ever could, and with wonderful beauty, in her poem, "The Concert."*

---

*From "The Harp-Weaver" and other poems by Edna St. Vincent Millay. Harper and Brothers.

"THE CONCERT"

No, I will go alone.
I will come back when it's over.
   Yes, of course I love you.
No, it will not be long.
Why may you not come with me?—
You are too much my lover.
You would put yourself
Between me and song.

If I go alone,
Quiet and suavely clothed,
My body will die in its chair,
And over my head a flame,
A mind that is twice my own,
Will mark with icy mirth
The wise advance and retreat
Of armies without a country,
Storming a nameless gate,
Hurling terrible javelins down
From the shouting walls of a singing town
Where no women wait!

Armies clean of love and hate,
Marching lines of pitiless sound
Climbing hills to the sun and hurling
Golden spears to the ground!
Up the lines a silver runner
Bearing a banner whereon is scored
The milk and steel of a bloodless wound
Healed at length by the sword!

You and I have nothing to do with music.
We may not make of music a filigree frame,
Within which you and I,
Tenderly glad we came,
Sit smiling, hand in hand.

Come now, be content.
I will come back to you, I swear I will;
And you will know me still.
I shall be only a little taller
Than when I went.

WILL EARHART AS PRESIDENT

> *More than a hint of the significance of Will Earhart's position in the field of Music Education is indicated by the fact that he was elected president of the Music Supervisors National Conference at the eighth meeting, for which he was host in 1915 in his home town, Pittsburgh Pa. As president, Earhart served through the ensuing school year, and his successor, elected at the rousingly successful convention held in Lincoln, Nebraska in 1916, was Peter W. Dykema. There is a smallish history to be recorded in a chronological report: This was the ninth year of the new organization. Will Earhart's predecessors in the office of president were, in sequence: Frances Elliott Clark, P. C. Hayden, E. L. Coburn, E. B. Birge, Charles A. Fullerton, Henrietta G. Baker Low, Elizabeth Casterton, Arthur W. Mason. Successors as national president in subsequent annual terms through 1920, following Peter Dykema's incumbency, included such illustrious music educators as Charles H. Miller, Osbourne McConathy and Hollis Dann. Probably all of these would support the statement, "And among the greatest contributors of this period was Will Earhart."*
>
> *This incidental interpolation has particular significance if taken into account when reading the material following, which comprises the original manuscript of Will Earhart's presidential address at the 1916 convention of his beloved professional organization.*

IT IS A SELF-EVIDENT truth that a wise system of education can rest only upon a wise discernment of the true meanings and values in human life. The value of any subject depends upon the power it may possess to elevate, strengthen and energize the quality of human life. This life is complex. We live in certain relations to great universal principles and ideals—spiritual laws—that shape our ultimate destiny and salvation. We live in certain human relationships

—as friend, brother, sister, husband, wife, father, mother—which are profoundly tender and noble, and which seem in their highest and holiest developments to merge with the shining values of the universal ideals. Again, we live in our capacity as instruments of utility to others; as workmen and clerks, hewers and builders, draughtsmen and mechanics, working busily in a busy world.

I have stated these phases of life in the order of their value; but of late there has come into the world a dangerous obsession with the third and lowest phase of life mentioned. Because the material phase of life is an immediate and outstanding necessity, we have let it obstruct the shining path of vision which opens upon more celestial vistas. We have even suffered ourselves to cherish the delusion that attainment of the spiritual depends first upon a thorough-going conquest of this material obstruction which, despite our efforts, looms ever larger in our path. It is a foolish hope. Our efforts only serve to increase and not to diminish the mass of material life. We do not see that salvation comes from turning aside from the portentous bulk and passing it by. Oriental wisdom saw our effort more closely. A Japanese, a member of a commission sent to investigate our occidental life, said, quaintly and with kindly irony: "Surely you Americans get everything done before you die; you work so busily."

The value of an educational subject, then, is proportionate to the power it possesses to elevate, strengthen and energize our lives. It is a means towards an end. But a means holds value according to the value of the end it moves towards, and not according to its mere efficiency. A machine for making bone collar buttons might be marvelously efficient, but bone collar buttons are not a prime necessity to a high and spiritual life. Similarly an educational subject may minister admirably to the advancement of certain phases of our life, and yet be refused high place because of the inferiority of the phase to which is ministers. And consequently the subjects that give us spiritual horizon, quickening of imagination and sensibility, breadth and sensitiveness of sympathy, stimulation toward high and idealistic endeavor, and a broad liberation of mind and spirit, are of greatest value. But in stating these qualities I have almost named these desirable subjects: Literature and the Arts. It is these that move the deep subjective moods out of which our moments of highest endeavor and human greatness are born.

I have permitted myself this general discussion because I wish to call your attention to the responsibilities that rest upon all of us to formulate some concept of the dignity and worth of our subject; and again in order to make clear a general trend that is manifest in our programs. This conference is committed by its program of the week first to an inquiry into the large values that music may hold—not to the professional musician, but as a live force in moulding the character and quality of a great, democratic people. Secondly, it investigates the relation of music, in a scheme of instruction, to other subjects, and its correlation to art instruction in particular. Only after such large orientation is given it, do the programs discuss, appropriately, features and methods of practice. I say this discussion appropriately comes last; for features and methods of practice are certain to be either weak or misdirected or blundering unless they spring from a clear and wise conception of ultimate ends to be attained. He walks falteringly or foolishly who has not a clearly defined and a worthy goal for his steps.

We do not need to indulge, here in our meetings, in self-glorification; we do not need to give ourselves false encouragement by speaking in hyperbolic terms of the greatness of our work; but there is value to all of us in recognizing the extent and richness of the domain which has gradually come into our possession. Our efforts are no longer restricted to the elementary schoolroom. The high school, which articulates with the adult consciousness of the community, has become a veritable gold mine in rich yield to our efforts, and the adult community itself is rapidly coming under our guidance for such inspiration as we can give. It is small wonder, with so large and attractive an opportunity presented to us, that our meetings show such buoyant enthusiasm, such conscientious endeavor toward progress, such eagerness to spring into action.

. . . I would point out that our professional organization has now come to a new period of development. I believe it is a safe assertion that throughout these earlier years we have valued the organization because of the instruction and enlightenment it brought to us. But now it is time for us to *give*, rather than receive—though in giving we always receive, also. We have learned our profession, we have formulated our faiths and creeds; pedagogically speaking, we are prepared, in knowledge and enthusiasm, for our individual tasks. Now the time has come to carry the faith to others.

CHILDREN'S VOICES AND MUSICAL ART

> *This paper, presented at the annual meeting of the sixty-first year of the Music Teachers National Association, Pittsburgh, Pennsylvania, December 1937, followed a demonstration by a chorus of children from the elementary schools of Pittsburgh, Mr. Earhart conducting. Reprinted by permission from the MTNA Volume of Proceedings for 1937.*

PERHAPS musicians will be indulgent if I begin by alluding to many well-worn facts. I do this, not because I think the audience is ignorant of them, but because the road around which the facts cluster is the most direct and appropriate one that leads to the view I have in mind.

The modern orchestra is, of course, the most comprehensive and pliant tonal medium that musical art possesses. Here we find the entire range of pitches satisfactory to the musical ear; any and every tonal color wanted; a vast range of intensities and volumes of tone; a diversity of parts that permits an infinite number of color combinations and the most intricate rhythmic and melodic weavings; the distinguishing characteristics that arise from generating and termination noises; and the distinctive types of phrasing that arise from the varied modes of operation peculiar to the instruments.

If we turn, now, from the orchestra to the mixed chorus we find the prodigality of resources sharply lessened. Every one of the resources mentioned, except that of sonority, has been greatly diminished. Four to eight parts supplant the twenty-three to thirty-six or more of the orchestra; and range, tone colors, idiosyncracies of tone production, and complexities due to many more parts being interwoven, all disappear.

As a further step let us consider the adult treble-voice chorus. The subtraction here of the male voices deprives us of another octave of compass; and the parts still further approach uniformity of quality. Four voice parts are possible, but their freedom of movement is restricted by the narrow compass within which they must move.

The treble-voice chorus composed of children is distinguished from the treble-voice chorus of women by additional diminutions in range, due to the loss of deep contraltos, and still more by losses in sonority and intensity. Besides these, many other differences of course exist that are of considerably greater importance than those we have named. But such other differences inhere in the mental and affective natures that lie back of the voices, rather than in the physical tonal medium itself.

In what kind of a world does a child live? That is the question we have to answer; and it is difficult because one removed by long decades of realistic living may not easily recapture or penetrate the mind and heart of a child.

Primarily we may observe that a child lives in a world far more limited in area than this extensive one which we adults know so well. Our world comprises a thousand distant theres-and-thens which are rolled up to make big and complex the present moment. In comparison, a child lives in a here-and-now. No large bulk of past experience looms over his present moment; and the future exists only in the most shadowy and unreal forecasts. His attention-span in relation to any item of experience in this limited world is short, his coordinating (or associational or integrating) power, slight. Accordingly he is flexible, pliable, almost fickle. At the same time he is minutely, acutely, sensitive to all that does break in upon his sensorium and gain his attention. Just as his skin differs from ours in its delicacy of texture so, we may imagine, do all his sensibilities differ from ours. We can withstand shocks as of sound or of light, that would be overwhelming to an infant; but he may hear and see delicacies which would not register with us at all.

With respect to the feeling which pervades a child as he lives and responds to such a world, it must be evident that it is not anthropopsychic. It requires many years of living before the child wishes to possess and command the world instead of merely to live in it and savor and enjoy it. In short, he enjoys trees, birds, stars, winds, waves, all tangs of life, as things-in-themselves—interesting, whether or not they be pleasurable or beautiful. And in this he is the true artist, in somewhat the sense that Taine has in mind when he says that an artist enjoys the play of a strong man's arm even though it be employed in knocking a good man down. Form and color, sound and odor are to him things-in-themselves, not symbols of some extraneous meaning.

As we try now to assemble and integrate into a music-making

medium the parts of the whole child that we have described—and do not imagine that I think he has no other parts—some repetition appears unavoidable. For it I again ask your indulgence.

After long years of experience in teaching music to children I have come to the conclusion that the child's fineness of sensory perception and his delight in exploring this fresh world of delicate sensory perceptions is the basic element for us to take into our thought. Consider the infant barely able to reach the piano keyboard, who holds himself upright with one hand while with the other he touches—or, it may be, pounds—now this key, now another, over and over again, for long minutes at a time. Every sound is an exploration, bringing with it a development of his auditory sense; and, moreover, the reaction he gives to each is a clear *aesthetic judgment*. Nor do the tones mean or signify or symbolize anything in terms of man's experiences in living. The tones are aesthetic absolutes: each is to be taken, and welcomed or discarded, for what it is in terms of the pleasure it gives.

It is unfortunate that we do not project our thought of the proper development of the child both culturally and musically from this starting point. But we have yet to learn that education can not be measured wholly in terms of bulk and velocity, but must be appraised also in terms of the amount of sensitive discrimination and taste that is developed. True, this fine discrimination and appreciation that the child applies to sheer tone represents such functioning only on the sensory level; but every exercise of delicate discrimination on any level, though it be no more than that of a tea-taster, develops some measure of culture that is not the less authentic because it is lowly. Were it not so in our music teaching, were we helpless to call forth all exercise of discrimination, taste, and aesthetic judgment until the child had grown to be a youth of high school age, our case would be indeed hopeless. Parenthetically, it may be that we labor under that very illusion. If we do, we lead the child to approach music with his rational mind, and to preoccupy himself first with knowledges, drills, and skills, believing that the aesthetic attitude will at some later date blossom forth of itself. Tragic mistake! Soulless piano pounders, jazz hounds, composers of futilities and homelinesses, although possessed of boundless knowledge and skill, remind us on every hand that knowledge and skill do not automatically synthesize into taste. No; the aesthetic ear should be cocked toward each and every tonal experience from the very beginning, even though it be but a single tone. How else, except in schools, would music ever ask us to listen?

Cultural result, then, need not wait, but can accompany the mind and fingers from the first note. And true musical appreciation similarly need not wait until the youth can become familiar with a twenty-page piece that bears an opus number. Below and beyond the realm of beautiful music stretches the realm of musical beauty; and sheer appreciation of the beautiful stuff of which music is made, namely *tone*, precedes, if it is not actually prerequisite to, the appreciation of the forms into which the stuff is woven.

To return, then, to our synthesis, the voice of the child in its lightness and purity, the mind of the child, in its detachment from the heaviness of human burdens, and the feeling of the child, sensitively responsive to the charm and interest of things-in-themselves, as they appeal in a curiously impersonal way to him, are all congruous, correlated and interpenetrative. The result is an instrumentality that is ideal for the projection of certain types and qualities of music. Among those types and qualities I would mention music that is short in form, that needs refinement and purity, not rugged boldness, and that voices disinterested joy, sorrow, exaltation, tenderness—as of blessed spirits—and not the poignant emotions of human tragedy. I would not be misunderstood. The child has very earthly and very real joys and sorrows. But those emotions of his have nothing to do with the way he feels about music, and if we should ask him to sing his feelings because he lost his skates or ask her to sing her feeling because she got mud on her hair ribbon, the idea would be regarded as most grotesque and comic, not only by the children themselves but, I trust, by us.

Here again the child is on the right road to the true sanctuary of music, which is where music as an absolute dwells. He is with Gluck and Mozart; not with Puccini, Wagner, and Tchaikowsky. The tragedies of earth are not yet his. Give him the poignant, fallen-angel tragedy, and he refuses to fall. He maintains psychic elevation and distance. This happens when he sings certain stark folk songs. He sings them with a curious detachment—is obviously more preoccupied with the song than with the literal occurrences with which the song ostensibly deals. But then, the folks themselves sing the songs in the same way. Bispham's singing of Lowe's *Eduard,* and a group of folks singing the same legend to a folk tune are on vastly different emotional planes. Similarly, children sing in

Pierné's *Children's Crusade* with none of that sense of heartrending tragedy that afflicts the grownups in the audience (by Pierné's unholy intention) at the thought of so many lovely innocents being drowned. It is just music to them, and it is not very childlike music. For childlike music, into which children can enter to the full, we must turn to Humperdinck. He knows where children live; Pierné does not.

A word about the specific effects possible in performances with a children's chorus—and I hope some of them were apparent in what you heard, for we sought them. Amazing tonal purity, greater than that of any other chorus, is attainable. Flexibility of voice and great ease in singing even the highest tones are further valuable characteristics. A certain musical—but not "emotional"—fervency and devotion, that are confined elsewhere to only a few fine artists, are often easily elicited. Dramatic values, on the other hand, can not be brought forth in marked degree. Within somewhat narrow limits a positive style can be achieved by emphasis in the articulation of consonants, and some degree of tonal coloration, as between open and covered and thin and thick (or round) tones, can be achieved. In the main, however, beauty rather than passion, and artless sincerity rather than formal artistic effects must be sought. The greatest passion of children is passionless *exaltation*.

WHO INVENTED MUSIC APPRECIATION?

> *"From the Turn of the Century" was the title assigned for the paper prepared for the Life Members and Founders Breakfast at the 1937 meeting of the Eastern Music Educators Conference held in Buffalo, New York. Will Earhart inadvertently supplied the above new title in a letter written some years later: "It is almost laughable that people are still fencing about who 'invented' the term 'music appreciation.' Who invented music? Who discovered God?"*
>
> *This book not being a history of music education, but a review of certain of one person's contributions to the field through his writings—and doings as thus exposed—the following short piece is offered for its revealing, if not historical, documentation.*

IF YOU WILL all come with me to the observation platform at the rear of the train, we shall look back on fifty miles of the landscape through which we have been speeding.

I cannot say that the first years of that half century are conspicuously clear to my own eyes, for during that time I did not have a comprehensive and integrated picture of school music in my mind. I was singing, as a student, "Hark! The Trumpet's Thrilling Sound," out of Loomis' *Progressive Glee and Chorus Book,* when the period began. A short time later I began to teach, but for a considerable time I saw only the few trees in front of me and did not see the forest.

While I was in Richmond, Indiana, where I went in 1898, the music appreciation movement got started. To my eyes it looks as though Mrs. Clark (Frances Elliott) and I started it; but a goodly number of Columbuses are always sailing around, and each discovers America for himself, lands and sings "Hail Columbia" (or whatever discoverers do), hoists his flag, and takes possession in the name of his particular sovereign. So I do not doubt that somewhere on our shores other appreciationists were landing. At any rate I started what I called a course in the critical study of music in Richmond in 1900. Mrs. Clark was teaching music history courses in Ottumwa, Iowa, at about the same time and in 1909 (she was a mere child then, but phenomenal), she discovered the usefulness of the phonograph and formulated definite courses. In that same year Clarence C. Birchard published four books of the *Master Musician's Series* in which Birge* and Earhart formulated the Richmond course. That series did not make the house of Birchard prosperous, but the books are still in print [1937]; certainly we did "appreciate" in those books. Since then, largely through Mrs. Clark's work, we have led the world in music appreciation.

Will you old-timers (that is a masculine noun; there are no old-timeresses) absolve me from self-aggrandizement if I tell of the features of progress as they came to me directly and not as somebody's research relayed them to me? You all know as much as I do about the nature and untold value of the work of the man I mention next—William L. Tomlins. He had all the earmarks of genius: large of body, large of heart, large of mind, he was one of those blue-ribbon specimens of humanity whom the Creator turns out only once in a while. He lifted singing to the plane of an esoteric and redeeming rite, and he spread its gospel over even more than our own shores. In 1918, or thereabout, his work came close to me, for he visited with us in our home in Pittsburgh for two or three days. Gradually he made clear to me that he wished to make me his spiritual legatee—bequeath to me his mission to carry on. How difficult it was to see, and to say, that I could not do it! Was I right? I could understand his system, but Tomlins was himself a system—of heart, mind, and soul—and did not merely have a system. I knew I could not become Tomlins, but must remain, bad as that might be, myself. Could someone else have done it?

Appreciation! Song! To what heights they have developed. But they almost pale in the light of the development of instrumental

---

* Edward B. Birge, long a close friend and professional colleague of Will Earhart.

music. Our school orchestras and bands incomparably surpass those of any other nation, and that progress has been largely made in the last twenty-five years. I am not sure that foreign nations wish to rival us in all features of our instrumental work. Perhaps they would regard our bands as too expensive for the cultural education students derive from them, but they may well envy us our orchestras. Yes, and now they must envy us our choruses, too, for our marvelous a cappella groups represent one of the noblest cultural developments that any school system has ever known.

Probably as much progress has been made in the last fifteen years as in the preceding thirty-five years. And latterly has come radio: for children in schools—Walter Damrosch, carrying his orchestra through the air as he once carried it on land to Western mining camps; and for the children's parents (who need it worse) —the Philharmonic Society of New York, the Metropolitan Opera Company, and many similar producers of great music.

And last week I heard that a teacher of music in an elementary school in Pittsburgh was late because her car broke down; the principal—who is a man—went in to her waiting class and played Beethoven and Mozart on the piano, and talked about the music, to the rapt interest of the children, until the teacher came. Now, in another fifty years . . . .

Well, perhaps we can have more without being better for it, but somehow I have faith that all this beautiful development must get us somewhere.

MAKING MORE OF
MUSIC IN SECONDARY EDUCATION

> *One of the earliest papers by Mr. Earhart to appear in official print was published in the "Proceedings" of the 1914 (seventh) meeting of the Music Supervisors National Conference held in Minneapolis, Minnesota. Entitled "The Place of Music in the Reorganization of Secondary Education," the paper, read at the convention for the author in his absence, excited a lively and fruitful discussion. It is printed in this book because it particularly reflects the circumstances and background of a significant development of the pioneering days of the organization in which Mr. Earhart had a prominent part. This comment is amplified and emphasized by footnotes one and three, pages 108 and 109, respectively. Footnote one quotes from Mr. Birge's "History of Public School Music," which in turn quotes from the 1917 Government (U. S. Office of Education) Bulletin No. 49, "Music in the Secondary Schools," prepared by Will Earhart and Osbourne McConathy.*

BEFORE LOOKING FORWARD to the place of music in a reorganized high school system, it may be well to cast a brief glance at music as it was in high schools in the past. Twenty years ago it consisted largely of chorus practice which ranged all the way from general assembly singing to proficient singing by carefully graded choral groups. In the main, however, the chorus hour was one of entertainment of a more or less elevated kind. Its chief artistic value was general rather than specific. If the students were dominated by the general mood of the song, as revealed by the text quite as much as by the music, and if they sang with right good will, albeit somewhat imperfectly to the ears of a musician, the school authorities were pleased and often the supervisor made shift to be satisfied. An hour a week devoted to this singing was an amount very generally favored. The pupils were supposed to receive, and unquestionably did receive, much benefit from the exercise, but it was seldom given any credit because the benefit was of a somewhat vague kind, varied greatly with the individual, and could not be accurately measured. It was an influence; but an influence and a definite educational advance must not be utterly confounded in our thinking. Once on a time educational grist was everything in the school teacher's eyes, and inspirational influence—character reaction—was nothing. Later, at times and in places, and with some subjects, character reaction became everything and definite educational acquisition sank to zero. Music was always prominent among subjects mistreated in this latter way, because of the extraordinary strength and value of its subjective reaction, and also because a certain measure of its reaction is obtainable on a low minimum of information. That a measure much greater in degree and more elevated in kind could be gained through greater knowledge, and that all influence needs firm foundationing in intellectual certitude to make it permanent and healthy—these facts were not seen. Then, too, there was not a high standard of musical scholarship, and the knowledge gained in the grades below the high school appeared to novices to be quite a large amount. For these reasons the promise given by music in the grades was not fulfilled in the high schools. Instead, the subject became atrophied there.

With the astounding increase in high school enrollment and the consequent building of elaborate courses, need for better treatment of music became obvious. It bore but poor comparison with other branches as to value, and its irregularities in the curriculum, compared with these others, made it troublesome. I cannot tell you how many letters I have received from superintendents and supervisors asking advice as to high school music, and saying in substance what one superintendent recently said to me in these words: "It looks to me like we would either have to make more of music in our high schools or cast it out altogether."[1] Almost all schools at

---

[1] Discussing this general subject Edward Bailey Birge, contemporary of Will Earhart, said: "It was shown that musically talented high school students who were studying piano or violin were frequently compelled to choose between leaving school and continuing their music, or remaining in school and dropping music. The combination of from one to four hours of practice added to three or four hours of study of other subjects made a prohibitively heavy load. The principle involved was clearly stated in the government bulletin, No. 49, prepared by Will Earhart and Osbourne McConathy, and entitled *Music in Secondary Schools*, as follows:

'We regard as untenable the assumption, expressed or implied, that any individual would be uneducated if he pursued three or four regular studies

some time have felt the pressure of this alternative, and the proper solution of it has been one of the chief concerns in late years of us who are supervisors of music. That music should not be cast out has been the determination not only of the music teacher but even of the superintendent or principal who has been troubled most by its desultory habits. Consequently we have seen a remarkable advance in the scope and strength of music teaching in high schools.

A definite stage in this advance was marked in St. Louis in 1912, when this Conference[2] adopted a report that advocated courses in Harmony, Musical History and Appreciation, Orchestral Ensemble and Chorus Practice in high schools, and added to that report an amendment favoring the granting of school credits for outside study of applied music. All who are interested in high school music should be, and all probably are, acquainted with the provisions of this report. Such acquaintance must at least now be assumed; and the purpose of this paper is consequently to outline the modifications or further developments that may possibly come about in planning anew for high school courses in music; these now to be fitted into a general plan of study which it is proposed shall be a reorganization of current plans.

For the information of some who may not be clear as to this latest work, a few words of explanation are given. The National Education Association some two years ago appointed nine members as a "Committee for the Articulation of High Schools and Colleges." This Committee later appointed, or secured the organization of, a number of sub-committees, there being one such sub-committee for each subject taught in high schools. Music was included.[3] Last

---

per year and added music to these, but would be educated if he pursued four or five studies each year and dropped music. We believe that this untenable assumption is due not to any active consideration of the question as to the place of music in an educational plan, but rather to a passive acceptance of traditional academic standards that are now outgrown and should be abandoned'."

[From *History of Public School Music in the United States*, by Edward Bailey Birge, page 166. Reprinted by permission of Theodore Presser Company, Bryn Mawr, Pennsylvania, owners of the original Oliver Ditson Company copyrights.]

[2] Music Supervisors National Conference, fifth meeting, St. Louis, Missouri, 1912.

[3] Will Earhart, was chairman of the Committee on Music of the NEA Commission for the Reorganization of Secondary Education. This fact gives weight to Mr. Earhart's paper in the light of the relation of the report to subsequent developments in the school music program and Mr. Earhart's participation as one of the leaders of the period.

summer the Committee applied to the NEA for permission for a change of name to "Commission for the Reorganization of Secondary Education," and this permission was granted. Meanwhile all the special committees, including the Committee on Music, had prepared preliminary reports. These have been printed by the courtesy of the Bureau of Education and may be secured by application there. The report of the Committee on Music, like the others, was tentative, but in its general features has been approved so uniformly by the members and by many musicians who, since its publication, have written the chairman, that we may safely assume these features will be retained. . . .

What will be the place of music in the reorganized plans and what may we hope will be its place in practice in high schools in the years to come? The outlook is certainly very bright; and since a meeting of the Commission in Richmond, Va., last February, the Chairman of the Committee on Music has felt greatly encouraged. Three developments at Richmond are of some interest. First, music was receiving no consideration by the Commission as a whole when the Chairman of the Committee on Music arrived at the meeting in which he was to speak. In a high school course of study spread upon a blackboard, music had no place within the sacred parallelogram, but was paranthetically mentioned below in a small corner of the board. The speaker on music, however, found that there was no lack of interest in the subject and no lack of respect for it *if it is made to consist of something more than mere experience of certain moods which poetry, the drama and all arts express equally well.* The suggestion that music is coherent discourse, that it demands attention, memory, co-ordinating power of mind if we would understand its beauty of design, the declaration that music is not and should not be all song or song-story, the plea for development of appreciation for the great instrumental forms, to be gained by a study of biography, history, form and aesthetics—these met with ready and sympathetic response. Again with reference to crediting in the high school applied music study under outside teachers, an amount of interest quite beyond the expectation of the Chairman was manifested. Many prominent superintendents were present and the expressions were almost uniformly favorable to giving such credit. Plans by which it might be successfully done were asked for, and the implication was plain that if such plans were forthcoming there would be little hesitation in adopting them.

We may expect, then, that serious study of music, that shall lose none of its delight but shall add nobler values to the old, will be a feature of high school practice according to the plans for reorganization. Crediting of outside study should also be a prominent feature of these plans. Finally these courses are likely to run through a six-year high school course instead of a four-year course, thus embracing the seventh to twelfth school years. This brings us to the third interesting development at the meeting of the Commission (for the Reorganization of Secondary Education) at Richmond, Va. With which I shall close.

The Reviewing Committee, of which Dr. P. P. Claxton, United States Commissioner of Education, is a member, held a meeting in which it developed that the special committees were questioning whether to prepare their recommendations of courses in such form as to fit them for adoption in high schools having four-year terms. It soon became manifest that the six-year division of the twelve school years in place of the four-year plan now in vogue, had many adherents. Indeed, the sense of the meeting was overwhelmingly in support of the six-year plan, as being more sound and in better accord with the psychological facts. These facts were summarized by Dr. Claxton in an interesting address, in which he said further, though it is dangerous to prophesy, he felt sure that ten or twenty years would see the widespread adoption of the six-year plan throughout the schools of the country. Such a prophecy is startling when one thinks of the enormous changes that would be brought about by such a reorganization of our school system. But if it is true that the ages of six and twelve mark points of change more exactly than do the ages of six and fourteen, then this reorganization should be effected whatever it may cost. Certainly we will agree that with regard to music there is greater difference in voice and in the nature of the text material between sixth and seventh years than between eighth and ninth; that it is true in other ways was the testimony of several authorities on the adolescent period.

Again Dr. Claxton summed it up well when he said that the years from birth to six represented the infancy of childhood, six to twelve, childhood itself, and twelve to eighteen the infancy of manhood; in which latter period a new set of school activities, administered in a totally different manner must be undertaken. Therefore, the high school is necessary at this age, with all the resultant changes in buildings, equipment and re-districting that this would bring about.

FACTORS OF MUSICAL APPEAL

This writing occupies more space than most of the Earhart papers in this book. "Factors of Musical Appeal and Responses of Pupils to Them," is the full title of the article, which deals with music appreciation, and which, the author admits, is somewhat "repetitive" here and there. The reader may not identify any such instances as faults of the author. The original manuscript, which occupied some twenty typewritten pages, could hardly be reduced without emasculation of what Mr. Earhart started out to say. Furthermore, the historical import of the fact that the writing took place in the period between 1928 and 1930 adds something to other connotations of this book, which have significance from the standpoint of historical and prophetic aspects—particularly as concerned with the development of vision and thinking in this second half-century of the existence of the professional organization of music education.

Opening with "The Roots of Music Appreciation," one of Will Earhart's last writings (1959), it seems appropriate to the character and import of the book to close with this essay, composed more than thirty years before and read at the 1930 convention of Music Supervisors National Conference in Chicago.

THIS PAPER has to do with appreciation of music. I must beg indulgence if it proves somewhat repetitive. In the course of many years of experience in teaching and in studying the teaching of music appreciation from many angles, the conclusion has been borne in upon me that our gravest errors in this field are due to disregard of some very plain and generally accepted truths of musical aesthetics and of the psychology of aesthetic response. From time to time I have unburdened myself of these convictions in papers like the present one. Now there is little need to restate the whole theory, for in these years there has been considerable progress. Let me recount the steps of this progress and then we can proceed to discuss what remains.

(1) The word beauty has come into our public school music vocabulary. I believe it first made its appearance in the Standard Course for Elementary Schools, adopted at a memorable meeting of the Conference in St. Joseph, Missouri. However that may be, it is a welcome, and, it seems to me, not altogether incongruous word for a body of music teachers.

(2) At least the wilder vagaries of programmatic "explanation" of music have become discredited. That is to say, there is some recognition of the fact that music expresses what we hear the tones do, when we listen.

(3) A superficial factual knowledge about music is no longer confused with feeling in sympathy with music.

(4) Tone-quality, in agencies for reproducing music and transmitting it, has been improved, with the result that we do not have to assume the presence of beauty in something that sounds unbeautiful. A measure of hypocrisy is thus eliminated.

Shortcomings in both our theory and practice that to my mind still exist are summed up in the series of statements following, that, after making, I shall wish to elaborate.

(1) The necessity of positively good, true tone as an indispensable aesthetic factor and as a pre-requisite to feeling the presence of other musical beauties, is not yet sufficiently recognized.

(2) The distinction between music as impressive and music as expressive is not taken sufficiently into account.

(3) The line of demarcation between an enlarging and powerful musical experience and the small graded experiences that make for peaceful penetration, so to speak, into the realm of music, is not at all clearly drawn.

(4) All of the factors that make for empathy are not weighed in.

(5) The close and essential relation between the aesthetic and the creative attitude is not sufficiently considered.

These statements do not in the least imply, on my part, a sweeping indictment of work that is done and that is being done. It is true that in the past, on occasions when I have been confronted with some particularly heinous crimes done in the name of music appreciation, I have been guilty of an almost murderous revulsion of feeling. On the other hand, I know that the subject is intricate and delicate beyond any other, and that thousands of strands, many of obscure origin, converge to make the fabric of appreciation. Moreover, appreciation is not an absolute quantity and is never completed. You and I, spending our lives with music, are conscious of gains or of changes in our appreciation from day-to-day and unceasingly. We differ, too, from one another in the direction, range, depth and sensitiveness of our appreciation, and our different states can not be defined or measured in strict terms. We may at least, then, grant that the task of developing appreciation in others is a delicate, obscure, and treacherous one—that can not be boldly and confidently undertaken in the belief that some concrete and standardized attainment dependent solely upon a course of study and some mechanical equipment will prove us to have been victoriously successful.

But let us discuss the alleged shortcomings.

Insufficient respect for the effect of tone alone (although tone-quality has improved) is yet doing incalculable damage to the cause of music appreciation. To anyone who will study the extraordinary effects upon us of sounds of all kinds, the extent to which we are dependent upon sheer sensory quality in music, will begin to appear astounding. I thought I valued this factor properly years ago, but its importance continues to grow constantly in my mind as my observations lengthen. We know, if we take a moment to think, that a Caruso with a cracked voice or a Kreisler with a cracked violin can give us no pleasure, no matter how fine the composition performed or what artistic graces are brought to its performance. Without exception the writers on aesthetics, too, from Gurney to Prall, support the facts by theory, in that they give place to sensory effect as an indispensable factor in aesthetic experience. Books on music appreciation, however, rarely make mention of it. They may rightly be excused, it is true, on the ground that they assume its presence as a matter of course, and could do little but name it anyway, since it is a factor not open to analytical discussion. But I fear their silence, coupled with their attention to form and forms—history, biography, national characteristics, and so on—has caused us to forget the importance of the sensory factor in practice; and to disregard it there is an entirely different matter. I have seen music appreciation lessons and, indeed, whole appreciation courses, ruined, distorted, made productive of only superficial knowledge and vast sentimental hypocrisy, simply because the tonal medium used was not in itself appropriate or captivating, or charming to the ear. Remember, there must be the actual *experience of beauty in the heart of the listener,* else all admiring comment by others draws forth at best only a complaisant, or a listless, assent that is without conviction. It is much the sort of hypocrisy we older people are led into when the doting mother would have us enthuse with her over the child of her heart, when the child has not captivated us in the least.

The point here is fundamental. It amounts to saying that unless and until we can bring to pass the conviction of beauty in the learner it is useless, or worse than useless, to expatiate on the factors that we feel have produced that experience in us. With small children such aesthetic experience is almost wholly response to sensory charm. With high school pupils, especially if they have heard and studied much music, it is true that the higher and greater values of organized discourse can be attended to although they must be sought behind a bank of inappropriate or ill-sounding tone. But even in such case there is danger of the appreciational process becoming aborted. The warmth that arises from sensory charm should be present to flow over and color the pleasure that arises from the recognition of beautiful ideas and thoughts. Lacking that favorable warmth the recognition of these latter may take on a cold, anatomical cast. The result then is that we arrive at an analysis that recognizes *what* is in the music but carries no feeling that rejoices *because* the features are there.

In this connection Prall distinguishes two kinds of attention, perceptive and intuitive, and has this to say: "In fact, if attention is characteristically perceptive and not intuitive, these further processes (i.e., aesthetic reactions deep within us) remain largely in abeyance, as when in musical dictation one hears so well as to write out accurately what was perceived through the ears and the sense for rhythm without in the least feeling the formal or sensuous or expressive beauty of the dictated passage."

Even in practical dealings with children, where the importance of the sensory is more generally recognized, many teachers, absorbed in a determined didactic purpose that will brook no restraint, close their eyes to clear, condemnatory evidence of error in this matter. I have seen children—polite children, who tried hard to behave properly—break into laughter when they should have been (according to the determined teacher's program) charmed; or drift away and look at the ceiling or at one another, or pick at some part of their clothing, when the music was saying important things but saying them in a tone of voice that lacked the vital element of charm. Yet those same children, a moment later, when the music quieted into a soft, mellow chord, grew still and wondering, as though the Pied Piper had passed before them; and those same children, still later in the schoolroom, raised their own slender lovely voices, modulated to charm their young ears, in a Schumann song that was as tender and small as they, and their absorption was a blessed thing to behold.

Now tone can fail in charm or in appropriate color in a thousand ways. It may be unsteady—as with so many singers and violinists afflicted with exaggerated vibratos and glissandos—or it may be impure, off key, meagre, thick, strident, hollow, unbalanced (as in a chord), thin, colorless, noisy. To each of these qualities we respond in feeling whether we wish to or not. And quite properly. Were sheer tones less emotional and enthralling, where would be the power and variety of appeals that reside in the multi-colored orchestra?

But let me adjure you to observe this same sensory effect, as often surpassing all other effects of music, upon an adult concert audience. I recently saw a somewhat sophisticated audience sit through some eight minutes of one piece of music. They were restless because, although the composition was good, the orchestra tone was unrefined and no pleasant sounds came to their ears. At the close a plain tonic chord, beautifully distributed, was repeated softly and then held through a swell with the inevitable subsidence into a pianissimo. In those brief closing moments the gathering became an audience. At the end they applauded heartily. The illusion was perfect. They had been pleased by a tonal effect and thought they had enjoyed a composition.

I could multiply instances indefinitely, for I have been analyzing the reactions of audiences at children's concerts (both when children were prepared and when they were unprepared) and at concerts for adults, and the reactions of all kinds of persons at all kinds of concerts (myself included) until I have accumulated evidence that almost persuades me that musicians themselves often cannot see the forest for the trees—or, speaking literally, cannot hear the music for the sounds. But there is no point in going further. It is enough to know that we err when we try to reach over a forbidding wall of sound to beauties that lie behind it. As Santayana says, "Now, a great sign of this hypocrisy is insensibility to sensuous beauty."

We err again, in much the same way, when we lead young folk to seek the *expression* of music instead of being receptive to the *impressions* it makes. The similarity comes again from the endeavor to reach behind what comes to our ears for some other content or meaning that we think lies there. Now, however, what comes to our ears is not sheer tone, but tones in patterns. But patterns, not less than single tones, have all kinds of personalities, so to speak, and affect us in myriad ways; and these different qualities of feeling are quite as indescribable in other terms as are the feelings produced by a clarinet as compared with a horn or bassoon. By its risings and fallings, its ebbings and swellings, its rhythmic runnings, loiterings, trippings, haltings and speedings, even a melody alone draws a portrait. That portrait differs from all others, is uniquely effective, and is simply a portrait of itself.

We have come somewhat out of the stage of programmatic explanation, but we still seek moods, meanings, expressional intention, back of music that is, as Burney put it, at once the expression and the thing to be expressed. The first evil of this is that it discounts the value of listening, attending, soaking up the music, and increases the amount of sentimentalizing done when music is heard—or we might better say, in this case, when it impinges upon the ears. Furthermore, it diminishes sadly the range of sensibility, because the categories of meaning into which it thrusts music are much less flexible and varied in character than the pieces of music themselves. For example—the most brutal example I can think of—we may hear it told that music in the minor mode is sad. *Sad,* I suppose, like "When Johnny Comes Marching Home," or the Overture to *Zampa,* or *Anitra's Dance*. What a falsehood! The infinitely flexible minor cramped into one dismal category! Most of us shudder virtuously. Nevertheless we continue to write program notes for children's concerts in which we employ a stock of almost equally imprisoning adjectives. Why can we not see that an adjective throws an enveloping blanket of mood over a whole piece that blurs its outlines, conceals its details, restricts its infinite variety, and can never be accurate? Do we not know that there are more ways of being sad—or glad—in music than there are adjectives in the dictionary? Is the music sad like Mozart, or sad like Beethoven or sad like Tchaikowsky? Is not sad music by Mozart more like his own glad music than like anybody else's sad music? Is the particular piece of music we are describing funereally sad, or tenderly sad, or tragically sad, or patiently or rebelliously or abjectly or bitterly or sweetly or pensively or cynically sad? Or *is* it sad at all, now that we think of it? Maybe it is truly in some mood that only music knows and has the word for. Anyway, when it is so beautiful, do you wish to spend your time thinking of it lumpishly as sad?

These foolish questions may have been unnecessary in bringing me to my point. Perhaps they imply that we should not try to interpret the music but only implant it. We may be filling the air with words while Brahms is waiting to speak. Or it may be that my friends Schoen and Bingham are right, and that one cannot *teach* appreciation but may spread a contagion of feeling by first catching it himself. In any case, my point is that no verbal description of meaning will say what the music says, for even when there is an avowed message which music would express, the impressions it creates while delivering the message are the richer part of its glory. Except for the value of these impressions, we should not need music at all, for the message could be otherwise conveyed. If we disregard the golden and wonderfully wrought casket, and throw it aside while we reach greedily for the lump of content, I fear we must lay ourselves open to the charge of lacking both musical and psychological subtlety.

Touching on the large musical experience as contrasted with smaller graded experiences, it seems clear that both have place and value. The pedagogical problem is to gauge their proportions properly. Just now this problem confronts not only music teachers but all teachers with burning insistency. The inventions of the last decade or two have enabled us to bring the large experiences of a lifetime into the schoolroom, and to bring them there with a richness, completeness and frequency sufficient to fill the whole time and attention, if we wished, of all the students. The outlook is stimulating; the educational millennium seems at hand. But we have to remember that while all great experiences are educational, all education does not lie in great experiences.

Education has been defined as analysis of experience. It may be retarded by over-analysis of a meagre experience or under-analysis of a rich experience. The range of experience, then, does not tell the whole story. Even more important is the perfect proportioning of the analysis. A Kant can become a master among the greatest minds without ever traveling more than forty miles away from his native Königsburg; and on the other hand a man may move among all the grandeurs the world has to offer and remain commonplace. There is no ground, therefore, for a blind faith that exposure to great experiences will bring about the millennium. Instead, the task that confronted the first teacher and that first confronts every teacher still remains. That task is, first, to bring about, at successive stages of an individual's growth, a set of experiences that provide possibilities of favorable developmental reaction: secondly, to employ all pedagogical tact, wisdom and skill to induce favorable reactions, and favorable reactions only.

Among the myriad experiences appropriate to any scheme of education, the enlarging, horizon-widening experience has an important and indispensable place. Its strongest feature is that it holds vast possibilities of stimulation, of general enlightenment. In this it contrasts so sharply with the humdrum of daily routine—often made more arid than necessary by reason of local pedagogical drouth—that it flames as a beacon of escape from dullness before the eyes of both teachers and pupils.

But there is danger in its very largeness and indefiniteness of stimulation. It may open a new world, but if the child cannot take full possession of some ground therein which he may use as his own pleasantly familiar playground, he has been in a way victimized. To expose him repeatedly to such strong allurements may finally create in him either a thirst for sensation or a callous indifference that betokens not lack of musical interest but lack of proper encouragement, a sophisticated cynicism, or, for the most talented, an early burning out of a fire that should have endured throughout life. I often wonder if the failure of prodigies to develop in later years is not due to just such a premature consumption of the whole stock of fuel.

I fancy I have seen signs of all the foregoing varieties of result among children who have been much 'fed up' on concerts and elaborate music and comparatively starved with respect to the simple but wholesome foods that should have constituted their daily diet. And it all seems so unwise and unnecessary. There is surely music at any and all times that is big for children or big for youths, without using the music that is big for men and for musicians only. Not but what this latter might and should be used, too, but only as the rare eye-opening experience, not to be analyzed, not to be definitized into points of learning, but simply to shake the sediment of routine into solution again, that it may perchance settle into new and crystalline forms. Such is the favorable reaction that should be sought; and to seek more is to create unfavorable reactions. The problem is the same with any grade of experience whatever, from the simplest to the greatest. It is to induce the reaction appropriate to the calibre of the experience, and that sort of reaction only. To let the small but potentially beautiful daily experiences, that should be embraced in entirety and be assimilated into rich growth, pass as humdrum incidents, is just as great a mistake, but not greater, than to overplay the absorptive powers of the student in relation to greater experiences. I repeat, the experiences should be in grade, and the amount and definiteness of analysis, as dependent upon the *kind* of experience, should be nicely gauged. The comparative frequencies of the one kind of experience or the other constitutes the remaining and less difficult phase of the problem.

To speak in concrete terms, the phonograph enables us to bring large portions of the music of the world into the schoolroom; broadcastings constitute an additional agency; meanwhile orchestra concerts for children have grown apace; and soon it will be possible to bring an entire opera into the school to be both seen and heard in a reproduction that is an excellent replica of the original. For some pupils, at some times, programs of some kind, in some proportion to other instruction, may well be employed from all these agencies. Even what might appear to be indiscriminate employment has its uses if pupils are not expected to exhibit an unnatural degree of comprehension and appreciation.

There is no reason, for instance, why a child of six years should not hear a symphony orchestra; indeed, there are some reasons why he should. In such a case I should be indifferent to the program, just so long as the music was good, because a child at that age is not prepared to make any reactions whatever to compositional content. I should not ask him questions or direct his attention to one factor or another for fear of spoiling his own direction of interest; but I should be pleased if *he* asked questions, and I should try hard to answer them. At the end of five or ten minutes—his sensibilities and attention-span would hardly permit his real musical experience to be longer, no matter how long he was kept within earshot—I should feel that a valuable and necessary but vague foundation for succeeding experiences had been laid, and should be content. Danger would arise if my pedagogical and uplift microbes stirred too vigorously and led me to want to reveal too much of what *I* felt to that defenseless youngster. This over-eagerness to uplift the children and masses is a constant danger. It is largely responsible for such over-stimulation, with its attendant dangers, as may sometimes be seen.

With either elementary or high school pupils the principle is the same. There is a steady growth, a laying of cell on cell in the spiritual make-up, that can best go on in the schoolroom, given a wise teacher; and there is the bursting sunlight of a new experience that can quicken life throughout all the cells. The two must not be set in competition but must work in cooperation. If our schoolroom work grows dull and unfruitful by comparison, we have failed as teachers and can claim strength only as promotors. If the large musical experiences fail to attract the children, to the point that they do not seek them of their own accord, we have missed either the right range of experience or the proper range of analysis. If, however, the regular basic school room work seems ever more musical and the extension programs ever more comprehensible as the two activities advance together, we are blest, because we have succeeded.

The Standard Dictionary thus defines empathy: "The ascription of our emotional feelings to the external object which serves as their visual or auditory stimulus." As Vernon Lee illustrates the meaning, a mountain rises because our eyes must rise to behold it; and it falls on the other side, because our eyes must fall to follow its contour. Similarly a melody rises or falls because of some correlative actions (infinitely more obscure, however, than those of the eye in the case just cited) that take place within us; and its rhythm is vigorous or quiet, again because the correlative actions within us are vigorous or quiet.

It is clear, then, that the nature of the action in use determines the emotional qualities of the thing heard or seen. The question I would raise next is this: How much of this action within us, which lends to the object whatever character and tang it may have, is congenital and arises out of our original constitution, and how much is due to powers developed in us by active dealings with life? To put it in concrete terms: How far does an infant who has never walked catch the tang of march music merely because he is a biped with *potential* duple leg-rhythm, as compared with the tang he catches after he has learned to walk? And we may as well extend the inquiry now and be done with it: If the infant became paralyzed before he walked, and never did walk, what would be the tang of martial music to him? What would be the tang of it, in that case, if he never saw other people march—or if he did see them march, but without music, and only heard march music separately? What would be the tang of it if he saw them march and heard the martial music in connection therewith?

If you see this as I do, you will agree that these queries strike at the very heart of the question as to how much of a vivid appreciation of music can be expected from an organism undeveloped by active dealings with life, and with life *in connection with music*. The whole question of developing appreciation from listening alone, considered without any reference to the student's active dealings with music, opens out at this point. Moreover, it is not a problem of appreciation without any experience, but is a problem of a correlation between experience and appreciation, implying that they are interdependent, that more or less definitely fixed proportionings exist between them; that they may rise or fall together.

Doubtless some responses are predicted in our nature in the beginning. I have already mentioned the extraordinary power of sound upon us. A sudden fortissimo sound causes an infant sharp distress and startles us adults. Pure tones, ugly tones, high tones, low tones, awaken reactions that have various emotional colors even to an infant. I think it is idle to say that any sort of action upon the world about him, or most rudimentary dealing with the production of tones, is necessary to fit the infant to exhibit these "appreciational" reactions. They must be implicit in the very auditory mechanism with its connections. One such connection may, it is true, be with vocal apparatus. Prall mentions the possibility of this, but does not speak in positive terms, since information is lacking. But while the possibility of some emotional reactions is thus provided for by the very nature of our organism, those that are implicit are much too meagre to account for the reactions that later become observable.

Do these later reactions, meaning now intuitive response to the myriad shades of emotional meaning in music, develop through hearing alone? The question is shrouded in obscurity because we cannot isolate the factor of hearing. While a child listens through the years he is growing and bodily changes are taking place. We can imagine that these changes produce an organism which registers reverberations more widely and delicately than the infant organism. This would mean that his innate musicalness is greater, but we know little as to that. The first difficulty in *knowing* arises from the fact that the child's mentality, his memory and coordinating power, have increased *and* have been dealing with an immense number of auditory experiences—which is to say that his hearing is becoming greater in itself and inextricably woven in with other senses; that meanwhile he has walked, run, danced, waved his arms, tapped on glass, metal, wood, bells, has cried, cooed, shouted, talked and sung, and has felt some way about it while he did so. In this last respect, for our present purposes, the child has become a producing musician. That is, he has established associations between certain feelings and certain rhythmic, tonal and melodic self-expressions.

In order to make fruitful investigations we need an assortment of different worlds. If we had a soundless world and could let children grow up in it, say to the age of sixteen years, and then introduce them into this very sounding world of ours and compare them with the children grown here, we might learn what part physical development alone plays in making the organism susceptible to feelings arising from music. Or if we had a world in which mental and physical development in many ways went on normally, but in which, at the age of two years, there was an arrestment of power for physical movement and power of producing tones by either vocal or mechanical means, and could then have musicians play to the subjects constantly (not incessantly) for some fourteen years— then we should have an opportunity for discovering what sheer continued hearing of music does, apart from locomotion and self-expression by tonal means, in making individuals understand and appreciate music.

Since we cannot have these curious experimental worlds let us consider a little more carefully what goes on in this real one. If you have played the violin, various tactual and muscular sensations —bow-pressure and weight, speed and firmness of fingering, string resistance to the bow at various distances from the bridge, etc.— have been connected with what you heard and with what you felt; that is, your emotional intention, while you played. When you listen to a violinist these sensations with their associated emotional colors arise to contribute empathic understanding. Is there a scintillant shower of tones that makes small technical demands? The emotional tone of the music is shallow, there is vivacity without depth. Is there a slow movement that is played with depth and intensity of tone? You feel the grip of the bow on the resisting string, close to the bridge, the pressure on the bow stick, the determined pressure of the fingers on a string that is being coerced to give up its last measure of expression. In short, your empathic power is conditioned not by auditory and rhythmic reverberations alone, but by other reverberations in your system that have come to join them through your experience with violin. It is doubtful whether a pianist or a horn player catches the "feel" of the violin music so quickly and surely as you do. Certainly one who had never made the most rudimentary attempt at singing or at playing any instrument would be less certain of the emotional intention. It is precisely lack of such practical associations, I think, that accounts for the tragically or ludicrously inappropriate response, smiles, untimely applause, silences, bewilderment, with which a lay audience receives the performance of a pianist, violinist, or other instrumental soloist. It is noteworthy that such inappropriate responses do not often arise in connection with singing, and this helps to prove the point. We all use our voices to some extent for emotional expression, and so know in a measure a sad voice, an excited voice, an exulting voice, a tender voice, together with the melodic lines and nuances that go with that mood-quality.

I should be unfair to truth did I not add that there can be, as we often have opportunity to observe, production of music without appreciation. Many who have little or no ability as producers appreciate music more truly and deeply than many who do produce it. The contradiction is an apparent one only. Some persons have much more imagination than others, and their obscure and unknown efforts in producing music reveal more to them than advanced producing ability reveals to others. So does a novelist know how life affects characters even better than some of the characters know. But granting equal, let us say mediocre, imagination in two persons, the one who learns to produce music will surpass in appreciation the one who does not.

Two eminent authorities may be cited as supporting the position I am maintaining. One is M. Jaques-Dalcroze. That rhythm and mood in music should be re-enacted by, and thereby made substantial in our organism is the thought at the basis of his great gospel. The other is Dr. John Dewey. His doctrine that interest and meaning do not inhere in an object but that our active responses pour content into it, seems to me to apply here.

We are wise, then, in developing participation in producing music to the admirable extent now apparent in our schools, and 1 believe we should make participation unanimous among our students so far as that can be done without coercion. On the other hand, the chasm that we have thrown between our efforts toward production and our efforts toward appreciation is deplorable. All of our singing and playing groups should steadily gain in appreciation, and all of our appreciation groups should sing and play. To listen to some one else's music is good; to listen to our own, and make it more and more worth listening to, is better.

My last point, the relation that exists between the appreciation and the creative attitude, is connected so closely with the preceding one that it needs only brief discussion.

Not long ago, I spoke on the subject: Highways and By-ways for Musical Pilgrims. The ensuing discussion turned for a time, as is inevitable nowadays, upon jazz, then later to ultra-modern music. At the time our Pittsburgh International Art Exhibit was in progress and all over the town there was much interest and discussion about it, especially in connection with some extraordinary ultra-modern works from many countries. Finally someone asked me: "Is there not a blood-relationship between modern music and modern painting? Do they not spring out of much the same psychological states and pursue the same aims? And just what are those aims?" I could only reply: "I regret that I am too ignorant to answer. In the case of music I believe I can penetrate the composer's feeling and divine his purposes. In art, I have had no instruction and cannot recall ever having made even rudimentary attempts at drawing or painting. Lacking that experience I find myself utterly unable to guess how a man feels when he lays paint on canvas in that way."

After what was said in the preceding section, it is evident that this incident might as well have been related in support of that proposition as in support of the present one. I wish to extend the thought a little way, however.

The creative attitude in music or in art, as conceived here, is not the endeavor to create original works. It is a commonplace in connection with music to regard performance as re-creation. Unless the performer puts himself back of the music and stands there at the side of the composer, sharing richly the creative intention and the creative thrill and interpreting it in terms of his own need for expression, he is a mechanician, not musician, and cannot be said at the time to be even an appreciator of music, much less an artist. The appreciative and the creative (or re-creative) attitudes are therefore one.

But just as the long series of mental states and the complex series of actions that go to make the violinist later move forward and up to join with and color his feeling about the music he plays, making it violin music; and just as some movement down those same paths of thought and action by one who is to listen and appreciate will, according to the vitality of his imagination, give the listener advantage in appreciative understanding of the violin concert; so will some movement down the paths of thought and action that are traced by a composer enable the listener to appreciate better what we may call compositional intention. This is the reason why we have found in Pittsburgh that the students in our harmony classes, where the work is based almost exclusively on original composition, often develop a rich and true appreciation more rapidly than do the students in our appreciation classes; and consequently we have developed one appreciation course in which composition of little pieces is the principal factor. It is the reason too, for our having an almost incredible amount of improvising and notating of original melodies and songs on the part of our elementary school children, from the kindergarten throughout the grades. Wherever that work is richest we find the interest in music greater, the singing more beautiful, the sight singing more fluent, the part-singing more finely chiseled. The practice has grown to such a point that an elementary school giving a school concert hardly considers itself entitled to a respectful hearing unless it includes a few songs composed by the singers themselves; and whole cantatas and operattas, or plays with music, are by no means a rarity.

Just recently I went to a school in a district that never has more than the bare necessaries of life and now is feeling the pinch of unemployment. I went to hear a whole group of Indian songs composed by pupils from third to sixth grades, as part of a project done in cooperation with the Educational Department of Carnegie Institute and Museum. I should have been prepared, after what I had heard in the past; but the beauty, the finely caught Indian character of those songs astounded me. They were evidently the children's very own, too. None of the music teachers in Pittsburgh could compose melodies so unsophisticated. Rhythms, cadences—and even modes in one case—that are not in our conventionalized minds were delightfully used. The children were in a mood that I can only call celestial. Such expressions as I saw seldom come into their eyes when they sing songs that someone else composed—and yet they sing those other songs beautifully, even hauntingly.

I think those children are likely to learn music appreciation!

The moral is to lead all pupils to sing, to play, to make up music, and to listen to much good music, as in concerts; but before you have them listen, be sure they have developed the organic appreciational apparatus to listen with, for ears alone will not suffice.

SECTION THREE

ABOUT WILL EARHART THE MAN

> Pertinent to the significance
> of the content of the previous
> pages is the personal and pro-
> fessional biographical data
> compressed into Section Three.

WILL EARHART—HIS LIFE AND CONTRIBUTIONS TO MUSIC EDUCATION

Report of a Doctoral Study, Reprinted with permission of The School of Education, University of Southern California, Los Angeles, California, 1960.

FELIX E. McKERNAN

Music Department, Occidental College

IT WAS THE PURPOSE of this study (1) to investigate the part which Will Earhart had in the development of music education from 1898 to 1956 and (2) to ascertain the nature of his contributions to music education.

Data compiled from published material of which Earhart was either the author or the subject was analyzed, synthesized, and arranged in historical and thematic presentation. Personal interviews with the subject were conducted, and correspondence with him was carried on continuously throughout the investigation in order to insure greater accuracy in both the reporting of the facts and the interpretation of his philosophy. Earhart's own evaluation of the investigation was then appended to the completed study.

♦

Earhart was born in Franklin, Ohio, in 1871. As a small child, he was drawn to music and showed early evidence of musical talent. As a high school student, he directed a church choir and played in a community orchestra and attained a considerable reputation locally because of his musical activities.

He was largely self-educated, both academically and musically, inasmuch as his formal education was terminated at the end of his junior year in high school.

His early aspiration was to become a professional writer; his career as a teacher was more or less thrust upon him by circumstances. His first teaching position was in Franklin in 1888, and during the next few years he taught music in both Franklin and the neighboring town of Miamisburg. In 1896 he became music supervisor in Greenville, Ohio where he remained until 1898.

As music supervisor in Richmond, Indiana, from 1898 to 1912, Earhart developed a public school music program which ran without interruption from the first through the twelfth grade.

He was one of the early pioneers in the development of instrumental music in the public schools. One of his first innovations in Richmond was the formation of a high school orchestra in 1898, when such organizations were almost unknown; under his direction, the Richmond high school orchestra became what was probably the first high school orchestra in the country to achieve symphonic proportions.

Harmony and musical history were established, at Earhart's request, as accredited electives in the Richmond high school curriculum in 1900. In 1901 he broke away from the traditional history course by changing it to a course in the critical study of music, or music appreciation, in which the students developed appreciation by taking an active part in the preparation and rendition of choral and instrumental works. By 1905 he had obtained accreditation for participation in the high school orchestra a full twenty years before high school credit was awarded, in general, for this activity.

Earhart projected the music program of the Richmond schools into the community by means of music festivals which involved the participation of children's choruses, a civic chorus of high school students and adults, and a civic symphony orchestra comprised of high school students and adult residents of the community.

The significance of the Richmond program, as it was pointed out by many of Earhart's contemporaries, lay in the development of musical culture as a direct and natural result of the public school education and influence; in the public ownership by municipal consent of almost two dozen musical instruments at a time when the precedent of using public funds for such purposes had not yet been established; in the permanence of the program itself, which continued year after year, without interruption, from first grade through adult life; in the demonstration by Earhart, as musical director not only of school children but of all the people gathered in Richmond's schoolhouses, that choral training was as feasible and as valuable in the modern city as it was in the pioneer community; in the provision of a more complete form of musical education in the schools, by means of which Richmond had shown the possibility of developing large and stable amateur organizations of a superior type; and in the accreditation which Earhart obtained for the study of music in the Richmond high school when no more than a half-dozen schools in the country allowed similar credit.

In 1912 Earhart was appointed Director of Music of the Pittsburgh public schools under a new state educational code which provided for the reorganization of the entire school system. From 1912 until his retirement in 1940, Earhart organized, developed, and administered a music program on elementary, junior, and senior high school levels in which every desirable phase of music education was given superior handling.

During his early years in Pittsburgh, Earhart standardized the music practices in the elementary schools and brought music regularly into every classroom in the city on a definite, scheduled basis, and he organized the high school music program to include chorus, orchestra, harmony, and appreciation. During the next few years he expanded the elementary school music program to include various levels of choral and instrumental groups, as well as music appreciation, listening lessons, eurhythmics, and class instrumental instruction. He extended the junior and senior high school programs to include various choral and instrumental groups, harmony, music appreciation, and the awarding of credit for the study of music outside the school. Creative musical activities were emphasized on the elementary and junior high school levels, and the composition of original melodies was encouraged in the senior high school harmony classes.

The music program ran without interruption from kindergarten through high school and was extended to the adults of the community by means of music festivals, public school demonstrations, adult evening classes in harmony, appreciation and musical theory, as well as choral and instrumental groups.

Earhart was an active member of the Music Educators National Conference for almost half a century. He was elected to the vice-presidency of the Conference in 1910, and to the presidency in 1915; in addition he served continuously as a member of the Research Council of the Conference from 1919 to 1944 and was twice elected to the Council's chairmanship.

His many contributions to the Conference included his early efforts to extend music to the high school and to broaden existing high school programs; to obtain the accreditation of music on an equal basis with other academic subjects in the high school curriculum; and to raise the professional standards of music teachers and supervisors. He continuously sought the encouragement of music as a vital force in education and in life and encouraged his fellow Conference members to establish their principles of music education upon a sound philosophic basis.

He was active in the school survey movement for almost two decades, during which time he conducted surveys of public school music practices on both city-wide and national scales.

As a teacher in higher education beginning in the first decade of the century, Earhart was frequently a lecturer in colleges and universities. In 1911 he taught the first course in instrumental methods offered by any school in the country, and he conducted courses in musical aesthetics on the college level at a time when such classes were rarely a part of the college curriculum. From 1913 to 1920, he was affiliated with the University of Pittsburgh, where he set up and administered the Department of Public School Music.

His published writings cover a span of more than fifty years. He was the author of four books: *The Eloquent Baton, Music to the Listening Ear, The Meaning and Teaching of Music,* and *Choral Techniques.** He is also the author or co-author of a wide variety of music materials covering practically every area of school music.

Earhart regarded philosophy, aesthetics, psychology, and the practice of teaching as component parts of one problem. He held that the affective life of the individual deserves fully as much attention as the intellectual and the physical, and that the value of the humanities and the cultural arts lies in their ability to develop in the individual a finer subjective, or inner, life. It was his opinion that the aim of all musical instruction in the public schools should be the cultivation of taste, appreciation, and discriminating perception of, and love for, the beautiful—without sacrifice of technical thoroughness or breadth. It was not his intention to make musicians of the students—it was his belief that what music does in the student is more important than what the student does in music—but to fit music in a wholesome way into the diverse lives of boys and girls until its leavening influence becomes an integral force.

In the teaching of music to children, Earhart stressed the fact that

---

* These books, published by M. Witmark & Sons in 1931, 1932, 1935, and 1937 respectively, are now out of print.

the child is in a sensory stage of development and that, from the beginning, music should be directed to the aesthetic ear and interest of the child as well as to his physical ear and rational understanding. In the belief that love of beauty is something that is caught rather than taught, he recommended that children be led very gradually and wisely from the stage of sensory response, in which they are subconsciously aware of the larger value of design, to a conscious recognition of musical beauty in its tangible form. He advocated that all technical advance in music by the student be immediately applied in the purchase of a corresponding amount of musical satisfaction and that the development of techniques be accompanied at all times by the immediate reward of musical outcome.

The effect of materialism and the scientific method upon contemporary society was regarded by Earhart as a tendency to evaluate every area of life, including the subjective life of the individual, in objective and quantitative terms in which pursuit of the beautiful is crowded out by material considerations. He believed that preoccupations with the scientific way of knowing—as the only way of knowing—inevitably reduced life to starkly mechanistic terms in which the life of the spirit is overlooked, and the richness and savor of life are lost. He maintained that much of the difficulty could be resolved if science would concede the same authority to religion and philosophy in their fields that they concede to science in its field; science need not accept the specific findings of either religion or philosophy, but only accept as valid the data and the mode of dealing with them that obtain in these fields.

In the course of his public school music career, Earhart repeatedly pointed out that music education is in need of a sound and articulate philosophy inasmuch as the philosophy which supports the arts is not grounded in, begotten of, or even confluent with current educational philosophy. After his retirement he continued to recommend that all action in music be in the service of aesthetic ideals; he strongly advocated more mature and more deeply musical experience for children in the elementary grades, in the belief that the work accomplished on this level has been inferior to that of the high school level; and he recommended that the teaching and learning of music go forward at every moment in a spirit of devotion and humble discipleship to something transcendently lovely.

MEMORIES OF WILL EARHART

On the Occasion of the Preparation for the Fiftieth Anniversary of the Class of 1911, Richmond High School

HUBERT S. CONOVER

Richmond, Indiana, September 24, 1960

FELLOW CLASSMATES: While we are gathered here, as a "curtain-raiser" to the fiftieth reunion of our high school class, it seemed appropriate to our chairman that I say a few words about one of the "greats" of the faculty of those days, Will Earhart. What I'm going to say is mostly personal. It is not a eulogy; it has to do with some of the things that Will Earhart did to put me and most of the rest of us in shape to enjoy life just a little bit more than we might have otherwise.

Will Earhart was a teacher, but he was a very great human being. He wanted to see that people enjoyed all the arts, not for the arts' sake, but for the people's sake; and he carried that mission to his death. He came to Richmond in 1898—about the time most of us were six years old—just starting in school. He was the Richmond Supervisor of Music, when supervisors of music weren't very common. He had gone to high school in Franklin, Ohio. He got booted out of the Franklin high school, due to a prank—and never went back. The next year he was invited to become the Music Supervisor in Franklin! After that he went to Greenville, Ohio, and then to Richmond. He was in Richmond until 1912, making a national name for himself as a music educator and community leader—and a national name for the schools of Richmond. He was at that time invited, after a search of the whole country, to take over a similar position in Pittsburgh, Pennsylvania, where they had had a difficult political situation in the schools for years.

Richmond was in a great turmoil as to whether it should let Will Earhart go or not. The Chamber of Commerce tried to make up a purse for him, to keep him in Richmond, but he felt the greater field was Pittsburgh and went there. In passing—that year I had just finished my freshman year in college and Will wanted me to go to Pittsburgh and take over one of the high schools. "I'm just a youngster," I said; "there are students as old as I am." "Well," was his reply, "there were students *older* than I was when I started out in Franklin." But, we had a family council of war and decided I should finish college. I said I would go to Pittsburgh afterwards, which I did in 1917, when I went to a school in Allegheny City.

Will Earhart's work in Pittsburgh brought the whole music system of the schools into focus as it had never been before.

In 1940, Will retired and went to San Diego, California, where he and Mrs. Earhart bought a beautiful home out near El Cajon, on the top of Mount Helix. They spent the next ten years beautifying the place, planting fruit trees and all sorts of exotic trees. Mrs. Earhart had a beautiful rose garden—and it was lovely. They worked as hard at that as he had in music before. They later moved to Portland, Oregon, where their son was in business. Their attractive apartment, where I visited them, had a big window that looked out over Mount Hood. The last several years prior to Will's death they lived in the Willamette View Manor—an ideal place to live. [At the time this is printed (1962), Mrs. Earhart is still there and very happily situated.]

Many of us have recollections of Will Earhart walking into Starr School, or one of the other Richmond schools—a medium-size man with a twinkle in his eye, wearing a little round black hat, and with a violin case under his arm. That was the highlight of the week, for me anyway. Later on at the Garfield School he amazed me when he taught classes there. He would play the violin, playing the alto and tenor parts at the same time, and singing the bass part. Of course there were plenty of students who could sing the soprano part, so he had the other three parts going on all at the same time. That was fantastic to me.

At the Garfield Junior High School Will started a little orchestra. I was a shy kid, and did not have nerve enough to go into the room where they rehearsed, so I'd poke my head in from around the cloakroom door and look at them and wish I could play one of those nice instruments. The upshot of it was that I studied cello and finally got so I could play and I was allowed to come into the high school orchestra. At about this time we had the May Festivals which Will conducted, and we had a wonderful chorus and we had the Chicago Symphony orchestra.

One of the times I remember was one year when Will was setting up the chairs on the stage at the old Coliseum—folding chairs—and when he stepped over one of them it threw him and he broke three ribs. That night he conducted the Brahms Requiem just the same.

Well, Will Earhart took me under his wing, and was my Musical Godfather in high school. He gave me a Berlioz book on conducting one summer to study. I read it and practiced before a mirror. That fall Will said, "Now come up here in front of the high school orchestra and try it." In those days we played things from Victor Herbert and Lehar. (We hadn't grown quite as long-haired as we are now given credit for having been.) We came to a grand pause; and I remember our director pinning my arms down to my sides—I had my hands up in the air. "If you don't want them to play, you get your arms down." Thus was forcibly demonstrated an important axiom, especially for a very green conductor. We went on and he let me, as well as other students, conduct the high school orchestra once in awhile. Well, so it went on, Will always encouraging us by trying to teach us more things than just music itself, as I said.

One time I recall he had a very great friend of his who was a nationally known music critic, W. S. B. Mathews, come down from Chicago and talk to the high school. Will invited me to sit on the Earharts' porch that afternoon, just to listen to those two men talk. Here I was just a young cub. Such things students do not forget. This broadening of horizons was the kind of thing that he tried to bring out with his students and in his teacher training too. I'll never forget one thing he told me that some famous musician said, "With amateurs, never play anything you can't make sound *as good as it is*."

Will always used to get into a dog-fight with Walter Damrosch when they got in the same room together, because, he said, "Damrosch taught people *about* music, instead of teaching them *music*." All those things have contributed to me in a way that I think has caused me to have more satisfaction out of being an amateur musician than I ever would have from being a professional musician.

Will was very much interested in the National Association of Amateur Chamber Music Players, which I helped organize. Now all that consists of is a directory which you carry with you, and if you're in let's say Columbus and you don't want to go to a bad movie that night, you get this directory out and look up the local names that are in it. Certain ones are marked with a star, which means that person is willing to call up his friends and round up a string quartette for you to play in. That's the kind of thing that meant more to Will than just learning out of books.

It was in 1908 that Will Earhart started the Richmond Symphony Orchestra, and the roster of that would be interesting; the first horn player was a barber in town. The other players were from many businesses, with a sprinkling of professional musicians. There were a number from the high school who played, as well. The first concert was at the high school—a free concert at the end of that season, and it was well attended. From then on, the Richmond Symphony had its place, and was finally brought in to play the May Festival programs.

Today there are hundreds of community symphony orchestras in the country. Now that is not any news, but it all started right from this sort of thing. That doesn't mean that the Richmond Orchestra was the first community orchestra, but the movement was fed by Will Earhart's disciples going out to teach.

I want to add a word here about Mrs. Earhart, whom many remember as the handsome young contralto in the Richmond Presbyterian Church quartet, possessed of a luscious voice and a charming and understanding personality. She was an active partner to Will, interested in all things cultural and artistic. The famous Stephen Foster Memorial in Pittsburgh would never have been brought to fruition without her vision and untiring work.

Although Will never finished high school and he never went to college, he was the best read man I knew. He was a tremendously deep student of philosophy and a philosopher himself. He could talk on any facets of philosophy, the arts, or aesthetics; but all the time he always had that little twinkle in his eye and he always enjoyed a good joke. And he loved and believed in people. His work lives on.

EARHART'S PROFESSIONAL RECORD

> *Data given here was in part compiled from the records in the Music Educators National Conference office, and in part with the aid of Mr. Earhart himself. The first portion of the listing pertains to posts held in the Conference.*

Vice-President, Music Supervisors National Conference, 1909. (Name changed in 1934 to Music Educators National Conference.)

Member, Board of Directors, 1912-1915.

Host to the MSNC Convention at Pittsburgh, 1915; there elected to the presidency for the ensuing term. (See page 96.)

Chairman, Committee on Compilation of Music Lists for School Orchestras, 1917.

Chairman, MSNC Educational Council (founded 1919), 1919-1921.

Chairman, MSNC Committee on Required Courses in Music for High School Students Receiving Credit for Outside Study, 1920.

Conductor Book and Music Review Department of *Music Supervisors Journal* (now *Music Educators Journal*), October 1922 through September 1936. Continued to supply occasional book reviews for the *Journal*.

Member, MSNC Educational Council, 1922.

Member, MSNC National Research Council of Music Education (successor to the MSNC Educational Council), 1923-1929.

Member, Committee on National Conservatory Movement, 1925-1930.

Member, Eastern Conference Committee on Statistics, 1927.

Conductor, All-Southern Conference High School Chorus, Asheville, N. C., 1929.

Appointed Editor of the *Music Supervisors Journal,* 1930. Could not accept the post but continued as editor of the Book and Music Review Department of the *Journal,* and served as editorial and professional advisor to the managing editor.

Chairman, Committee on Resolutions, 1930-1932.

Chairman, Music Education Research Council, 1931-1936.

Member, Committee on Music Administration, General Committee for the Century of Progress Exposition, Committee on Music Appreciation, Committee on Contacts and Relations, 1932-1934.

Member, Editorial Board of *Music Supervisors Journal,* 1930-1936.

[Note: In 1930 instead of appointing an editor as first planned, the Executive Committee set up an Editorial Board to supervise editorial content and general editorial policy of the official magazine. Will Earhart was a member of this first Editorial Board. Edward B. Birge, the first Chairman, for all intents and purposes, had the responsibilities of an editor until he resigned in July 1944.]

Chairman, Council of Past Presidents, 1932.

Member, Committee on Experimental Projects in Music Education, Committee on Music Education Broadcasts, 1936-1938.

Member, Music Education Research Council, 1938-1944.

Public Schools: Supervisor of Music, Franklin, Ohio, 1890-1896; Miamisburg, Ohio, 1894-1895; Greenville, Ohio, 1896-1898; Richmond, Indiana, 1898-1912; Director of Music, Pittsburgh Public Schools, 1912-1940.

Other Educational Posts: Northwestern University, teacher and superintendent of summer music schools, 1900-1912. University of Pittsburgh, lecturer in music, School of Education, 1913; professor, 1918. Carnegie Institute of Technology, School of Applied Design, lecturer, 1916-1917; professor, College of Fine Arts, 1921-1940.

U. S. Bureau of Education: author of *Music in the Public Schools,* Bulletin No. 33, 1914. *Music in Secondary Schools,* Bulletin No. 49, 1917 (joint author). San Francisco Public Schools, Survey and Report, Bulletin No. 46, 1917. Elyria, Ohio Public Schools, Music Survey, Bulletin No. 15, 1918. Public Schools of Wilmington, Delaware, Music Survey, Bulletin No. 2, 1921. Memphis, Tennessee Public Schools, Music Survey, Bulletin No. 50, 1919.

University of Rochester: Music Survey with relation to Eastman School of Music and the Public Schools, not published but on file in the office of the University of Rochester, 1920.

Congden: *Music Reader* No. 1, 1909, No. 4, 1918, joint editor and contributor words and music.

American Book Company: editor, *Art Songs for High Schools,* 1910.

Oliver Ditson Company: *Music Student's Piano Course,* joint editor, 1918.

Degree: Doctor of Music, University of Pittsburgh, 1920.

Organizations: MENC, American Society of Composers, Authors and Publishers, American Society of Aesthetics, American Musicological Society, Music Teachers National Association, National Education Association, Musicians Club, Phi Delta Kappa, Phi Mu Alpha Sinfonia, Unity. Many others, city, state and national.

BIBLIOGRAPHY

IT HAS BEEN POINTED OUT that Will Earhart's formal schooling terminated before he graduated from high school. Yet, he was one of the best educated men in the music education profession in the first half of this century. The articles collected in this book abound with references to literature and philosophy. The accompanying bibliography is presented to readers who may wish to follow Will Earhart's plan of self education by reading in some of the works that contributed to his thinking.

Bacon, Francis. *The Advancement of Learning.* Edited by W. A. Wright. New York: Oxford University Press, fifth edition, 1900.

Bell, Clive. *Art.* [1914]. New York: Capricorn Books, Putnam's Sons, 1959.

Bergson, Henri. *Creative Evolution.* Translated by Arthur Mitchell. New York: Henry Holt & Co., 1911.

Birge, Edward B. *History of Public School Music in the United States.* Boston: Oliver Ditson Company (Presser), 1928.

Burney, Charles. *An Eighteenth-Century Musical Tour in Central Europe and the Netherlands.* Edited by Percy A. Scholes. London: Oxford University Press, 1959.

————. *An Eighteenth-Century Musical Tour in France and Italy.* Edited by Percy A. Scholes. London: Oxford University Press, 1959.

————. *A General History of Music, from the Earliest Ages to the Present Period (1789).* With notes by Frank Mercer. New York: Dover Publications, 1957.

Conant, James B. "Role of Science in Our Unique Society," *Atlantic Monthly,* 181 (March 1948), 47-51.

Croce, Benedetto. *Aesthetic.* New York: Noonday Paperback. 1956.

————. *The Essence of Aesthetic.* Translated by Douglas Ainslie. London: W. Heineman, 1921.

Dewey, John. *Art as Experience* [1934]. New York: G. P. Putnam's Sons, 1959.

————. *Reconstruction in Philosophy.* Boston: Beacon Press, 1957.

Durant, Will. *The Mansions of Philosophy.* New York: Garden City Publishing Co., 1934.

Goodhart-Rendel, Harry Stuart. *Fine Art.* Oxford: Clarendon Press, 1934.

————. *Architecture, Engineering and Sculpture.* A Study in the Philosophy of Design. Newcastle upon Tyne, 1947.

Gurney, Edmund. *The Power of Sound.* London: Smith, Elder, 1880.

Henderson, C. Hanford. *Education and the Larger Life.* Boston: Houghton Mifflin Company, 1902.

Hopkins, L. Thomas. *Integration, Its Meaning and Application.* New York: Appleton-Century Co., Inc., 1937.

James, William. "The Energies of Man," *Memories and Studies.* New York: Longmans, Green and Co., 1911.

Jaques-Dalcroze, Emile. *Eurhythmics, Art and Education.* Tr. by Frederick Rothwell, ed. by Cynthia Cox. London: Chatto & Winclus, 1930.

Jung, C. G. *Psychological Types.* Tr. by H. Godwin Baynes 1923. New York: Pantheon Books Inc., 1959.

Kwalwasser, Jacob. *Exploring the Musical Mind*. New York: Coleman-Ross Co., 1955.

Langhans, Wilhelm. *The History of Music in Twelve Lectures*. Tr. by J. H. Cornell. New York: G. Schirmer, 1886.

Lee, Vernon. *The Beautiful*. Cambridge: Cambridge Univ. Press, 1913.

——————. *Music and Its Lovers*. London: G. Allen & Unwin, Ltd., 1932.

Lowell, James Russell. *The Function of the Poet*. One of twelve lectures at the Lowell Institute. Boston, 1855.

Mathews, W. S. B. *Music, Its Ideals and Methods*. Philadelphia: Theodore Presser, 1897.

Maupassant, de, Guy. *Complete Short Stories*. Ed. Artine Artinian. Garden City, New York: Hanover House, 1955.

Mearns, Hughes. *Creative Power*. The Education of Youth in Creative Arts. 2nd rev. edition. New York: Dover Publications, Inc., 1958.

Meumann, Ernst. *The Psychology of Learning*. New York: D. Appleton & Co., 1913.

Millay, Edna St. Vincent. *The Harp Weaver*. New York: Harper & Bros., 1923.

Münsterberg, Hugo. *The Principles of Art Education*. New York: The Prang Educational Co., 1905.

——————. *The Eternal Values, Part III* "The Aesthetic Values." Boston: Houghton Mifflin Company, 1909.

Neuhaus, Eugen. *The Appreciation of Art*. Boston: Ginn & Co., 1924.

Prall, D. W. *Aesthetic Analysis*. New York: Thomas Y. Crowell Co., 1936.

——————. *Aesthetic Judgement*. New York: Thomas Y. Crowell Co., 1929.

Puffer, Ethel D. *The Psychology of Beauty*. Boston: Houghton Mifflin Company, 1905.

Reid, Louis A. *A Study in Aesthetics*. New York: Macmillan Co., 1931.

Ribot, Théodule Armand. *Diseases of Personality*. Chicago: Open Court Publishing Company, 1895.

——————. *Essay on the Creative Imagination*. Chicago: Open Court Publishing Company, 1906.

——————. *The Psychology of the Emotions*. New York: C. Scribner's Sons, 1897.

Ruskin, John. *Seven Lamps of Architecture*. New York: Noonday Paperbacks, Farrar, Straus, and Cudahy, 1961.

Santayana, George. *The Realm of Essence* (Part I of *Realms of Being*). London: Constable and Company, Ltd., 1928.

——————. *Realms of Being*. New York: C. Scribner's Sons, 1942.

——————. *The Sense of Beauty*. [1896]. New York: Dover Pub. 1955.

Schoen, Max. *Psychology of Music*. New York: Ronald Press Co., 1940.

Taine, Hippolyte Adolphe. *Lectures on Art,* first series. Translated by John Durand. New York: Henry Holt and Co., 1889.

Tolstoi, Leo. *What is Art?* Translated by Maude. Indianapolis, Indiana: Bobbs-Merrill Company, Inc., 1960.

Tomlins, William L. *Song and Life*. Boston: C. C. Birchard and Co., 1945.

Toynbee, Arnold. *Study of History*. New York: Oxford University Press, 1947, 1957.

ARTICLES IN THIS VOLUME

SECTION ONE

Value of Man's Non-Utilitarian Interests

I.	The Roots of Music Appreciation, 1950 (Author's Preface to this portion on page 9)	PAGE 11
II.	What Is Music For?, 1950. (Author's introductory statement on page 23)	25
III.	Congenital and Changing Acquired Interests, 1960. (Author's introductory statement on page 35)	37

SECTION TWO

A Selection of Articles Previously Published, 1914 through 1938

Largely taken, unless otherwise indicated, from the annual publications of the Music Educators National Conference. (The Yearbooks, and the preceding Journals of Proceedings).

A Quest for Basic Principles, 1926	47
The Values of Music, 1920	58
Musicianship and Mental Development, 1931	62
The Integrated Educational Program, 1934	72
To Justify or Not To Justify, 1931	80
Is Music in Danger of Losing Its Identity Through Integration?, 1937	84
Fundamentals In Music Values, 1927	90
Will Earhart as President, 1916	96
Children's Voices and Musical Art, 1937	99
Who Invented Music Appreciation? 1937	104
Making More of Music In Secondary Education, 1914	107
Factors of Musical Appeal, 1930	112

SECTION THREE

About Will Earhart The Man

Will Earhart—His Life and Contributions to Music Education, by Felix E. McKernan, 1960	130
Memories of Will Earhart, by Hubert S. Conover, 1960	135
Earhart's Professional Record	139
Bibliography	141
Articles in This Volume	143

143 /